How to make it in the ROCK BUSINESS

How to make it in the ROCK BUSINESS

Mary Wilson

COLUMBUS BOOKS
LONDON

To Tony and our first-born, Gilmore, who developed and grew along with this book and was born with a good deal less effort.

First published in Great Britain in 1987 by
Columbus Books Limited
19-23 Ludgate Hill, London EC4M 7PD

British Library Cataloguing in Publication Data

Wilson, Mary
How to make it in the rock business.
1. Music trade——Great Britain——Handbooks, manuals, etc. 2. Music, Popular (Songs, etc.)——Great Britain——Handbooks manuals, etc.
I. Title
338.4′7′780420941 ML 3790

ISBN 0-86287-316-9

Typeset by Facet Film Composing Limited, Leigh-on-Sea, Essex
Printed and bound by The Guernsey Press, Guernsey, CI

Contents

Acknowledgements

My thanks to all the people in the music business who were kind enough to spare me some of their valuable time, including: Terri Anderson, Mark Ballabon, Clive Banks, Tony Barwood, Ed Bicknell, John Blake, Barry Blue, Brian Bonnar, Mick Booth, Chris Briggs, Brian Carr, Stuart Cosgrove, Paul Crockford, Peter Dadswell, Les Davidson, Rob Dickins, Simon Draper, Anne Dudley, Joan Eades, Roy Eldridge, Nick Fleming, Neil Ferris, Charles Gillett, Derek Green, Shaun Greenfield, Ian Haring, Tony Harris, Mike Hawkes, John Henry, Tom Hibbert, Peter Holt, Nigel Hunter, Tony Hutchinson, Paul Jenkins, John Kennedy, Jonathan King, Paul King, Steven Lenhoff, Steve Levine, Alan Lewis, Roger Lewis, Billy Livsey, Ron McCreight, Ian McNay, Daniel Miller, Martin Mills, John Moreton, David Munns, John Myer, Anne Nightingale, David Panton, John Peel, Chris Peters, Hugo Pow, Peter Reichardt, Jim Reid, Mark Reilly, Annie Rosebury, Martin Rushent, Tony Satchell, Red Scarlet, Jill Sinclair (the Tube), Jill Sinclair (ZTT), Rick Sky, Curt Smith, Clive Stanhope, Tony Stone, Tony Stuart, Jazz Summers, Meo Thompson, Len Thorpe, Phil Waller, Sara Ward, John Walters, Carol Wilson, Paul Wilson, Andy Woollascroft, the Icicle Works, James Wyllie.

M.W.

CHAPTER 1

The dream

At a co-ed just outside Liverpool, four youngsters met secretly at the back of Block A. One side of it was well soundproofed so that music lessons held there would not disturb the geography teacher in action next door.

Lessons weren't due to be held there for a couple of hours, and the four conspirators were each meant to be playing games. But all had registered sick.

One of them had borrowed the key to the music rooms. That gave them two whole hours to rehearse and talk about 'The Vision'. Next Sunday was the big day, and they had a few things to straighten out. They had been practising here for the last few weeks – unheard and unnoticed by anyone so far.

'The Vision' was the name they had decided upon for their group. The five members of the band were Vince, who sang and had played lead guitar for three years; Simon on drums; Violet of the raucous voice; Iona on bass guitar; and Winston on keyboards.

They had known each other since childhood. Their parents all lived close by. And for years they had shared a dream of following in the footsteps of their heroes the Stars – four local boys made good.

The kids' parents had grudgingly bought them their first instruments – second-hand, of course. They had grimacingly put up with the sounds of the novice musicians struggling to come to terms with the unknown, and finally given them permission to play together in a garage one family owned. When the neighbours complained, the parents said they were 'old and fuddyduddy' and should give the youngsters a chance. 'You never know what might come of it,' said one mother. When the locals complained over and over again, the infant group was banned from the make-shift rehearsal room. That's when they discovered the chance of using the school's music room.

Vince wrote some of the songs. He thought they were great; not all the others agreed. As a compromise they mostly played songs written by the Stars, with Vince's songs splattered around when they thought he would kick up too much of a fuss if they didn't.

They were a democratic little band. The one who shouted loudest and longest got his or her way. They weren't at all bad musicians, either. Some of their friends, whom they considered close enough to be able to hear what they played without slagging them off too much, were of the same opinion. Mind you, to know four people who were in a band was pretty spectacular. Perhaps they might one day be as well-known as the Stars. They were everyone's heroes in those days.

And now it was only one day to go to their first public gig. Please, God, don't let the teachers find out about us now . . . not until after Sunday.

The gig in the local pub had been quite easy to arrange. Vince's dad spent many an evening chatting to the landlord while quaffing his best bitter. He had never let a band play there before, but it was a big room, business was slack and Vince wouldn't let his dad rest easy until he had persuaded the landlord to give it a go: just one night, to see what happened. He wouldn't pay them anything, just give them a few free drinks. He wouldn't have much to lose, and if they were any good – well, the pub might just make enough to be able to give the group a few pounds.

On the day, the kids arrived before opening time. The landlord was cleaning the tables. He had moved them around to make a good-sized space for the band in one corner of the room. They had hired a small PA for the night, which Vince had brought in his car. The other band members had each brought his or her own gear. Amazingly, they had all arrived on time.

They plugged themselves in and played a few notes. 'Christ,' said the landlord, 'does it have to be so loud?' Vince thought about explaining to him that was half the normal volume they played at, but stopped himself. It was their first gig, after all. They would just have to play a little more quietly. They'd turn up the amps gradually as they went along; that way people wouldn't really notice.

The landlord disappeared behind the bar. He wasn't so sure about this any more, but it was too late. Several people at lunchtime had been asking about the evening's event – they were looking forward to it. Better than looking at the wife for an hour over a half-empty glass of beer, trying to think of something to say, or listening to her nagging.

The evening had gone well. Only a couple of the regulars had complained, but they complained about most things anyway. The general opinion was favourable.

The landlord asked Vince's dad if the band would play there every week. Vince's dad thought it was a great idea. If the boys were paid a little money, that might stop Vince pestering him daily for cash.

Unbeknown to the band, the third week they played at the pub an A & R man for one of the big record companies was in. A friend of his was a local who had told him about the Vision one evening. Only recently the A & R man's company had allocated him quite a large budget to spend on developing a new band – if he could find the right one – so he was eager to see anything recommended to him.

The gig had been a particularly good one. No one had broken any strings, the amplifiers hadn't blown up (they really were on their last legs) and the audience had been enthusiastic. The A & R man found out who was in charge of the band and had a quick chat with Vince's dad. Had anyone else shown interest in the band? What experience did they have? Could he speak to them tomorrow?

Vince's dad was over the moon. As soon as the man had gone he told the band the news. Could this be it? The big chance, and only a few weeks after playing regularly.

The next day dragged on and on. Vince sat glued to the telephone but it never rang. At 5 p.m. he went to bed. There obviously wasn't going to be any phone call. He'd heard how record companies operated and this sounded typical. Build you up, promise the world and drop you down again.

At 6.30 his dad was thumping on the door yelling that there was a phone call for him. Vince was down the stairs in one bound. It was the A & R man. Could the band come up to London next week to have a chat with him and the A & R director? If they got on well, the band would be offered the chance to make a demo tape. Yes, he knew they had no money. The company would pay for the demo. They wanted to hear what the Vision sounded like on tape.

*

Vince and his mates were up early on the arranged day. Should they wear the gear they wore for gigs, or just look casual? They opted for their stage gear – not that it looked much different from what they wore every day.

They climbed on a train to Euston and caught the tube into the record company's West End offices. It was very alarming. Plastered over the walls of the reception were dozens of gold discs – five of them belonging to the Stars. It was their company too – that must be a good omen. The receptionist was all dolled up, painting her nails and paying very little attention to them. Didn't she realize she was looking at next year's hit band?

They sat in reception kicking their heels for half an hour. What was the delay? Had he changed his mind at the last minute? What the hell, maybe they should go home now. It must be just a dream, he must have mixed them up with another group. Just then, the buzzer went on the receptionist's desk. She waved them over. 'He'll see you now. Up the stairs on the left, second floor, Door 1.'

After a half-hour chat, the band realized that the company was really serious. They talked about doing a demo in the studio. The A & R man had really liked one of their songs and they told him they had a couple more which they thought could be hit material. He would spend £2000 getting the group into shape, developing their image, having photos done. If the demo turned out well, they would sign contracts for a single and an album, with options for further records. The full contract would be for five years, with an advance for each record. The first advance would be £75,000, with royalties at 12 per cent.

The Vision walked out two hours later in a daze. Their first deal, and it was all so easy. After a few minutes of stunned silence, the bragging started. They'd always known, hadn't they, that they had it in them? This was going to be a great year.

Four weeks later they were in a rehearsal studio. The A & R man introduced them to a well-known producer. They spent one long day running through four songs. It had seemed so easy when they played them live. Now they had to play parts separately, sing unaccompanied and get their timing spot on.

It wasn't easy, but by midnight the A & R man and the producer seemed happy enough. To the band, what they had done all sounded very odd, but they presumed the producer knew what he was doing. The next day they went into the recording studio, The producer wanted to go straight for masters. Four days later they emerged.

The next day was a revelation. The tapes sounded good, so good they could hardly believe it had been them playing on it. The A & R man came in, very excited. 'This is it,' he said. 'I knew it when I first heard you. You are going to be mega.'

A week later they were back at the record company, where they were given a thirty-page contract and advised to get a lawyer to look at it. Vince read a couple of pages without understanding much of it beyond their own names. They would take it to a cousin of his who was a solicitor. He hadn't seen anything like this before, but at least he understood the legal jargon. He told them they could sign it happily. Next day the deed was done. Everyone shook hands, and a bottle of champagne was opened.

An hour later, the band was on its way home. We really are going to be stars, thought the Vision, glazed with excitement and champagne as they made their way to the rather grubby London digs the A & R man had found for them. That night they dreamt of fame, money and adulation.

Two months later their first recording was virtually wrapped up. They had been back in the studio for the final overdubs on the songs the producer had chosen for their début single. They were beginning to feel like real stars. They didn't even have to lug their equipment around: a roadie called Alf had been assigned to them.

Vince had thought he was going to lose his voice at one time; he'd never sung so much in all his life. But a couple of days' rest had done the trick. The master tape would soon get its final mix before being turned into the Vision's first single.

They discussed sleeves with the record company's art department and after much to-ing and fro-ing came up with a simple but striking design based on a hazy picture of the group itself. They met the company plugger, who liked the single and said he'd be doing his best to get it played. A date was decided on for the release: another two months away.

They didn't know how they'd be able to wait that long. Meanwhile, however, the record company had got them an agent who had organized quite a few gigs – much better than the pub where they first started out – supporting a couple of big names, and this kept them busy. They had to hire a van to get around, and Alf came along to help. With their advance they had bought new guitars, a drum kit and three synthesizers. How much they had spent so far they were not sure, but they felt it was all under control.

The support gigs had elicited a few reviews and their local paper had run a story on them. 'Sudden Fame for Local Kids', the headline ran.

The two months passed. The plugger had worked hard and a couple of evening Radio 1 programmes picked up on their single two weeks after its release. Then they were told the record was going on Radio 1's 'B' list. They couldn't believe their luck. The record had been sent to all the music press and they bought every paper printed. Three had picked up the record and given it an OK review. One even enthused about it: 'One of the best tracks I've heard from an unknown band . . . the Stars had better watch out.'

Six weeks later, the record hit the charts. It crept in at 198. A week later it was 74; three weeks after that it reached the top twenty. It was now on Radio 1's 'A' list and friends were ringing up continually to congratulate the band members.

They had made it. Eight months after their first tiny gig, they were stars. And the single was due to be released in Europe and America to coincide with their first US tour.

The Vision would soon be international superstars.

THIS WAS ALL A DREAM . . . NOW READ ON.

CHAPTER 2

The dream exploded

If only it were that simple – walking into a gig with little or no hassle, getting a deal with the first record company that comes along and having a hit with the first record!

The reality is that everything is likely to be a battle: each stage will take several goes to get right, and there will certainly be quite a few hiccups, if not disasters, along the way.

The popular music business today is a very different animal to what it was in its infancy – or even twenty years ago. In the 'fifties and 'sixties pop music was mainly for the young. The new teenagers had a medium which they could call their own and enough disposable income to spend on its related merchandise. Rock music was detested by most people over thirty years old. That in itself gave it an attraction, an extra appeal, which raised it from being just a fad to an important element in the newly developing youth culture.

Today, pop music – or rock – has a far wider audience. It is enjoyed by almost everyone, from tiny tots to trendy pensioners, by royalty, bus conductors and business executives alike. Although some of its more extreme forms – punk, for instance – may have been looked down upon by the older generation, popular music has lost its shock value, probably for good. It is now generally acceptable – part of the established leisure scene.

Pop music is more respectable now than it has ever been. It is an interest to be encouraged in the young, not frowned upon.

For many, becoming a rock star would seem to be a relatively simple way in which to make a fortune. Little do they know... but, of course, every year brings new names to the scene, and some of them, against overwhelming odds, do make it.

The odds on succeeding are no more than one in a thousand. If you decide to go for it, you'll be competing against some 30,000 new artists a year, and as well as talent you'll need enormous persistence and determination. Enthusiasm, commitment and the will to help yourself will also be useful attributes, as will an ability to pick yourself up when you fail to clear the hurdles. If this doesn't sound like you, maybe you should think twice about this particular career.

The music business is very big business. In 1986 67.4 singles worth £76.1 million (wholesale value) went into UK record shops, together with 52.3 million albums worth £140.6 million, 69.6 million cassettes worth £152.1 million and 8.4 million compact discs (CDs) worth £56.5 million. Exports brought a revenue of over £60 million. Britain also earns in excess of £350 billion per year in royalties from the success of British artists in the USA.

Highly organized and efficient though the business is, it also has a failure rate higher than that of most other businesses, in terms of return on expenditure. Major outlay often demands virtually instant success from artists and extremely hard work once he or she starts to 'take off'; the strain and stress of being constantly on show, and on peak form, can take a heavy toll of the young and inexperienced. No wonder we so often read of rock stars becoming addicted to drugs or drink, burning out or collapsing from mental and physical exhaustion.

Too many bands are trapped into a mayfly existence: they make too much money too quickly, lose impetus and fall into obscurity. Everyone wants to know those who are successful, then things change and suddenly they are nobody again. In this business you have to be prepared to face the very lows as well as the occasional high.

But for all the pitfalls and hard times there is still a fortune to be made by that lucky few. If you are talented, go about it in the right way, are aware of the man-traps – created by your own and others' schedules and aspirations – *and* Lady Luck smiles in your direction, you might survive.

CHAPTER 3

How the music business works

How does this huge machine operate? The following pages describe how, in essence, the different sections of the business function. Each is treated in greater detail later in the book.

Incidentally, where the text refers to bands it usually means solo artists as well, for many in fact operate like a band, the main difference being that they have to find musicians to accompany them. In the case of a band, decision-making and money are, on the whole, shared equally, while a solo artist has to take the decisions for himself, or herself, and pay musicians for their services.

A solo artist may of course operate entirely on his or her own, maybe accompanying himself or herself on the piano or with an acoustic guitar – or, alternatively, plugged into a bank of machinery. Often musicians start out as part of a band (possibly in the belief that there's safety in numbers) and only decide to go solo much later in the day, when their confidence has built up.

One now-successful solo singer remarked: 'I was singing with bands for many years and never, ever thought of myself as a solo artist. It was only when I had worked with several writers and several bands that someone suggested to me that I go it alone.'

Your first springboard, then, is likely to be in the context of a band – but even if it isn't, you will find the business operates in exactly the same way.

THE RECORD COMPANY

The function of the record company is to record artists and release those recordings – singles, albums, cassettes or compact discs – for sale to the general public. The company will press as many copies of the recording as it deems fit, at its own expense, and promote, market and publicize the record in order to secure sales. Within the company are various departments dealing with different parts of this process.

The purpose of the A & R (artists and repertoire) department is to find and develop new acts. It is also involved in pre-production and in developing the recording careers of its artists. These last concerns often leave A & R staff little time to scout for new talent. But, of course, new acts are the lifeline of a record company as much as the established artists. The difference is that successful artists bring money in now, while new acts *might*, or might not, do so in the future.

The distribution and marketing department is concerned with getting records to the wholesale and retail outlets. The sales force has to convince the shops (and therefore, ideally, be convinced themselves) that your record is worth stocking. Once it is in the shops it is up to the public whether or not it sells. For this reason it is worth staying in the good books of this department by not interfering with or upsetting the sales force. If, however, you have good reason to believe that it is not doing its job properly, the correct course is to discuss this with your manager, if you have one, or to speak to the A & R department. If you can, get to know some of the senior sales reps; get them on your side and they will do their best to sell your record.

If you are with a small independent label, it will use an outside distribution company or that specific arm of a major record company – in which case you will not be able to approach the sales force directly. You would have to talk to your contacts at the record company if you were unhappy about distribution.

The press and promotion department exists to make the media, the trade and the general public aware of your record, using radio, television, newspapers and magazines, advertising and posters to do so. Although the latter seem to get ripped down as quickly as they are pasted up, they can have a local effect, especially if you have a hard-core following, by alerting your fans to your new record, video or impending live performance.

This department will liaise closely with all other parts of the company, your manager and yourselves. How much time it spends on you depends how much importance the company places on you as a whole.

The legal department will prepare your recording contract and will liaise with lawyers outside the company as necessary.

The royalty department deals with the administration and distribution of royalties to each artist on the company's books. Its staff calculates to the last penny how much each has earned in both the UK and abroad.

PUBLISHERS

The function of the music publisher, which has changed considerably in recent years, is primarily to protect the writer's copyright interests. The first Copyright Act to make it illegal for anyone to perform someone else's work in public without making a royalty payment to the composer/songwriter was passed in 1911.

Until the 'sixties the main part of a publisher's business was to print and publish sheet music of his clients' work, charging so much per copy and passing 50 per cent of the profits to the composer/songwriter. The decline of sheet-music sales has been caused largely by the growing popularity of other forms of entertainment, such as television, computers and videos, and the concurrent decline in the numbers of people able to read music and play an instrument for home music-making purposes. Now sheet music represents only a very small part of a publisher's job; it is produced mainly for the top forty, and sometimes not until a number reaches the top ten – although compilation books, or 'folios', of songs, still sell very well.

Nowadays the publisher's prime task is to collect royalties on behalf of his clients and pass on the agreed percentage of that amount to them: usually 60-70 per cent. The publisher may be expected to 'work' the song, that is, send it to singers, record companies and so on, in the hope that they will 'cover' the song (record it), and encourage the use of his clients' material in commercials, on radio and television (including the new cable and satellite television channels), videos and films. Every time that a song is recorded, played on the radio or television or used in a film, for example, a royalty is due. It is up to the publisher to make sure that these royalties are collected in full.

MANAGERS

Initially, your manager might be someone in the group, or a friend, who has a head for business administration and organization; alternatively, you might decide to look straight away for a professional manager who is already experienced in the music business.

A manager's job is to deal with the business side of your career. He should take all the worry about practical matters – arranging gigs, dealing with agents, record companies, etc. – off your shoulders, so that you, the performer, can concentrate on being creative. While you are a brand-new band, he might well help you decide on which songs to play at a gig and how to improve your public image.

A professional manager can act objectively on your behalf. He should obtain the best deals he can for you, wheel and deal for you and generally do his best to promote your career.

He should work for *you* – not the other way round. He should not interfere with your creativity, unless you ask him to, and he should not take it upon himself to push you in any direction you do not wish to go. He will expect to take about 15-20 per cent of your earnings (usually gross earnings, i.e. before any deductions) from music; and he should earn that percentage, not just sit on his backside while you do all the work.

Beware of the manager who only talks about getting you a large recording deal, without considering how you should work towards that goal or how your career might progress thereafter.

A good manager is worth every penny; a bad one is worse than not having one at all.

AGENTS

Agents are purely concerned with your 'live' career, booking you gigs and tours, although for a large tour they will probably pass on much of the work to a tour manager. They take 10-15 per cent of the fees they obtain for you from the promoter. For pubs and the smaller clubs agents are unnecessary, but once you reach the more important circuits you will need an agent, firstly because the larger venues will only deal with agents, and secondly because you will never have the time or expertise to do it yourself.

PROMOTERS

Promoters, using their own money and resources, set up gigs and tours. They hire the venues, agree to pay a fee or percentage of the 'gate' (entrance) money, or a mixture of the two, to the artists, and they organize publicity.

LAWYERS

Lawyers should be involved every time a contract is offered, and quite often even before that if a new group is looking for a recording or publishing deal. Over the last decade some disgracefully unfair contracts have been brought to court and huge sums of money awarded to the wronged artist. One of the results of this is that no record or publishing company of any repute will even sign an act whose contract has not first been looked over by an independent lawyer.

ACCOUNTANTS

Accountants should also be involved very early on in your career. You may not think that as an unknown artist you need someone to look after your money, but not only can success hit you faster than you think (if you are one of the lucky ones), contracts signed when you are unknown remain in effect when you have hit the big-time, so the wording of the financial clauses of your publishing or recording agreement is crucial. An accountant will be able to ensure that the terms are fair, not just for immediate purposes but for a possible time in the future. For example, you will have to decide whether to sign as a partnership or as a limited company, which will affect your earnings when you begin to make money. Your accountant will advise on this decision in the light of current tax laws.

CHAPTER 4

Getting started

If you are serious about the music business, you must ensure that you have something to offer all the people from whom you expect support – the people with whom you'll be working in the business, and the listening public. You can't do this without effort, and the number of chances you get to make good are limited. If you turn into an also-ran, you'll find it practically impossible to crawl back. Give yourself the best chance by getting things right from the very beginning. Step one is to rehearse . . .

REHEARSING

Back rooms, schools and village halls are fine for rehearsing when you start out, but once you begin playing regularly you will need to investigate the availability of proper rehearsal rooms.

Until the early 'eighties all rehearsal studios tended to be tacky, dirty and devoid of ancillary services. There are still plenty of these around and many bands are quite happy to rehearse in them, but if you want something better, there are now bigger, smarter studios offering more civilized conditions. This means easy access to the premises, good monitors, equipment which works and, preferably, the right ambience. You should be able to utilize the time you hire purely for rehearsal, not waste half of it waiting to get into the studios or trying to make equipment work. And it's more conducive to work if the staff are friendly and helpful.

While a cheap room can cost anything from £3 to £5 an hour, the smarter studios cost from £40 a day (a day could last as long as 14 hours, remember) to over £100 for the biggest rooms, which may have recording equipment as well. These prices should include the monitor system. In 'low' times you can sometimes negotiate cheaper rates, even if the hirers originally told you there were no discounts. If you are free to rehearse during the day, or if you are making a longer booking – say, a week or longer – you should be able to get a cheaper rate. If you are hiring equipment from the studio at which you are rehearsing, you should get a discount on that, too.

Do bear in mind that it can often be difficult to get rehearsal space, especially at short notice. It's no good trying to get in somewhere two days before a gig. A lot of bands book up regularly at their preferred times, which limits the time available for others.

The advantage of the bigger and more expensive rehearsal rooms is that they can offer all the basic facilities and more. You will be able to unload your gear outside the premises and move it into a clean rehearsal room, at the time booked, without any problem; you will not have to wait for the previous group to clear out first, and you will find microphones and PA, if included in the hire fee, set up and working (or, if they don't, someone on hand to put them right immediately). The staff will also be able to help if *your* equipment breaks down, lend or hire you replacement gear, and sell you anything from gaffer tape and guitar strings to mikes and drum-sticks.

There will probably be a café of some sort on the premises to provide you with on-the-spot sandwiches and hot food while you are rehearsing, which saves you time you would otherwise waste in having to go out to find something; rehearsal-room cafés also provide bands with a chance to meet other groups and make business contacts, and to find out what's going on in the business generally.

Decent rehearsal studios should be able to offer different-sized rooms at different prices, with the largest one capable of being used for 'showcases' – performances for people within the business. These are one way of bringing yourself to the notice of A & R people, especially if you are based outside London.

Showcases can work better than live gigs, because you have the opportunity to set up in your own time and get used to the room. Bands sometimes book the room for two days, one for practice, one for performance. You know the equipment is going to work, and that if anything should break down it won't be the end of the world because it can be replaced or mended at once. Also you can bring in some friends for support, or to create a live atmosphere, if you prefer playing to an audience.

Most important of all, you can be in control of a very important day in the life of your band. You are not at the mercy of a pub manager or coping with the limitations of a pub environment. It can be difficult to persuade A & R people to attend a gig far away from their base, particularly late at night or on Saturdays and Sundays. A showcase provides you with the chance of inviting them at their own convenience, to pleasant surroundings, and you can arrange for individuals to come at set times rather than all at once. Overall, a showcase enables you to stack the odds in your favour.

You may decide that for the purposes of your showcase, or for making a demo tape, it would be as well to hire one or more session musicians in the interests of time and efficiency, or perhaps to deepen the texture of the sound you are creating; or perhaps one member of your band is relatively inexperienced and although he performs adequately when playing live it could be worth your paying for an experienced musician when professionalism really matters. The cost of a session musician could well be saved simply on the time you might otherwise spend trying to get a track right.

If you do not know any good session players, ask around or register with an agency such as Nu-Line, which puts bands and musicians together. Nu-Line has about 7000 people on its books, about one-third bands, two-thirds individual musicians. There are two rates for bands. If they are semi-professional, it will cost them £12 per 20 contacts per type of musician (e.g. drummer, keyboards-player or guitarist). A professional band (one with a record company, or one that works full time) will be charged £20.

The music papers are a good place to look for rehearsal rooms, as is the *Music Week Directory*.

HIRING EQUIPMENT

There are so many hire companies nowadays, all over Britain, that you can shop around for the best price. But apart from a good price, you need to know that the equipment is OK and you should not have to reserve equipment too far ahead. Most places prefer to be given a couple of days' notice, but usually end up dealing with panics – groups needing something in half an hour! If they've got the gear, then there's no problem.

With microphones costing about £5 each, plus VAT, including a stand, and a 400-500-watt PA – quite adequate for most pubs – £40 a day including mikes, but not transport, you should be able to cover the hire costs if enough people attend the gig.

MAKING A DEMO TAPE

Ten years ago you had to go into a studio to make a demo tape, unless you owned an expensive reel-to-reel tape machine. As studios in town became increasingly expensive, new ones began to spring up in rural areas. As technology improved and home recording equipment became more sophisticated, high-quality portable studio equipment – four-track, eight-track and sixteen-track machines – became widely available, and is now easy to rent. There are enough competing companies for the prices to be quite reasonable.

You could in fact make a demo tape at home which is good enough to be a master and present it to a record company as the finished item. The company may take it if it passes muster, though it may need tarting up by a producer. You might be able to do a one-off deal either for an album or a single, and if it should reach the charts you will then be in a very strong position to negotiate a long-term deal. Very soon, after all, we will have digital home recording gear, which will make it very easy to produce near-perfect tapes to present to record companies. But remember that the best recording equipment in the world can only preserve what it 'hears': if the basic sound is not right, you could be wasting your time. Hiring one or two professional session musicians could help (see page 24).

RADIO SESSIONS

Another way of obtaining a demo tape, if you are lucky enough, is to do a session for radio. ILR, BBC local radio and Radio 1 record live sessions and if it goes well you could buy the tape (a listening copy) for private use – taking it round to record companies, publishers and so on. The tape won't cost very much and will mean that you probably have a more professional-sounding tape than you would if you had recorded it yourself. At the time of writing, for example, a BBC listening cassette copy costs £17.25, a tape £40.25.

The group or its manager has to write a letter requesting the tape, explaining which session a copy is needed of and why (e.g. to play to managers, agents, etc.), and stating that the request is made on behalf of the group and with its permission, and to sign an agreement that it is to be used for private purposes only (not to make records from). This is the BBC's way of safeguarding the material, which could otherwise be used for commercial purposes by unauthorized parties.

You might put down four tracks for a *Janice Long* session, for example, and although you may not end up with the best musical quality – especially if you are not very experienced – a good sound and feel could be enough for a record company's A & R department to take an interest in you.

When doing a radio session, you need to be well rehearsed and know exactly what the producer wants. You might only have a few hours to put the tracks down and the producer will expect you to do it as quickly and professionally as possible: taking the time to get things right should be done beforehand in private practice sessions, or when *you* are paying for the studio.

To take part in a radio session you need to be a member of the Musicians' Union (MU). You will be paid the standard MU rate for the session, at present £75 per musician. You can be present for the mix and know what your contribution is going to sound like when broadcast.

Some groups make albums out of their radio sessions,

and BBC Radio Enterprises occasionally issues radio-session compilations.

Capital Radio sessions are similar, and although major record companies have to pay up to £250 per track for use on an album, the fee is negotiable for very new bands.

If you *do* use a radio session as a demo tape, remember that it will have that broadcasting station's name on it, which could go against you if you have recorded a Capital session and want to send it out to Radio 1, or another independent station, or *vice versa*.

SENDING TAPES TO RECORD COMPANIES AND PUBLISHERS

Making tapes for an A & R department, producer or manager is different from making a demo tape which will eventually be turned into a record. In the latter case you have time to build up the song, but a promotional tape has to get straight into the song. After all, yours will be one of hundreds the company receives each week, so it has to catch the attention immediately. You may envisage a single with a long, melodious, moody intro – but that is no good for a promotional demo tape. It is the first few seconds that count. Put your best two or three songs down on the tape, with your strongest song first. Time is at such a premium that the recipient may not even listen to the last song, or, if he/she does, may have lost concentration, particularly if the first two songs were weak. The company will be looking for a possible hit single, a song with possibilities, rather than playing proficiency.

Very few unsolicited tapes get anywhere. This is generally because they are not good enough. If you have been working long enough to be able to produce a good sound and a possible hit song it is more than likely that you will have made contacts during that time who will recommend you, so you will not need to send in a tape 'cold'.

An A & R director of one of the major record companies observes: 'You tend to get the more serious possibilities through contacts because the artists have done their research and more work. Contacts are just a way to get your tape raised to the top of the pile.

'Unsolicited tapes tend on the whole to be poor-quality and presented in an unacceptably amateurish fashion. Most front-room demos are not good enough, because you really can't get vocals across or achieve a good presentation in such circumstances, but they are OK for publishers. Rather than try to economize by making a demo at home, you should go to a small studio.

'Sometimes we provide £1000 for a band to produce a good demo, but only if it is recommended by someone whom we trust.'

If you do not think you have reached the appropriate stage to approach record companies, another idea is to send your tape to local DJs and clubs. Let them try the tapes out and see what reaction they receive. Clubs will play tapes and, provided the response is favourable, might well recommend you to a big company.

Although a brilliant song, badly recorded, is unlikely to be ignored, it must shorten the odds if it doesn't sound as if it had been recorded in the bath. As one A & R person puts it: 'Old tin cans don't sound as good as a decent recording, but that's not to say I haven't signed a band sounding like old tin cans. But I do feel the band is probably more dedicated if it's bothered to make a respectable demo.'

It is important to present your demo tape well in the visual sense, too. One that is clearly marked, well packaged up and sent to the right person will get much further than a tape with just a scribbled name and address on it which is stuffed into an old envelope and sent just to the record company. Even smartening up the case with coloured pens, for example, could make that first impression a little bit stronger.

Never send your one-and-only tape (make a copy) and make sure your name, address and telephone number are on the tape, letter, biography – if you send one – and any other piece of documentation. These items can easily be separated; the A & R person could be stuck with a superb tape but have no idea to whom it belongs.

If you know you have got something worth selling and cannot get a major record company to take interest, then go to an independent and try to get a one-off deal. That will serve to start the ball rolling, although you may receive very little money. At least you will get your first record out, and once you get plays and coverage in the music press you are more likely to be able to tie up a long-term deal.

At the moment, when there is very little outstanding rock music around, any group that is brilliant will get picked up eventually. So persevere: don't get dispirited if you have no response from the people to whom you send your tape; keep on sending it and eventually, if you persist, you are unlikely to be overlooked – provided you have something to offer.

Disappointment is part of the development of any band. If you cannot take the knocks at this stage of your career, you might as well give up. Don't expect miracles; don't expect to make it overnight. Most groups have been around for years rather than months before they come to the attention of a record company, and the experience and professionalism they acquire in the meantime never do them any harm.

One music journalist suggests: 'If you want to keep artistic credibility, go for an independent. If you want to make money, go for the majors. There are too many bands nowadays out only for making millions. They seem to relegate the music to the background. Lots of bands get too greedy. Too much weight is put on getting the best deal. Frankly, most groups should be glad to have got one. Just keep the length of the contract, the number of years, as short as possible, so you can move companies if you get successful, or renegotiate with your original one.'

SENDING TAPES TO TELEVISION AND RADIO PROGRAMMES

Before sending a tape to a programme, work out whether your music fits into that particular programme's format, then check the producer's name and send a neat, well-organized, professional-looking package of record and biography. The latter should be typed, clearly and concisely expressed, and include points which might alert the producer's attention – gigs, local following, major record company interest, if any. If the programme includes interviews, add anything which may strike the producer as good material for a different or amusing interview. If the programme never includes interviews, or only ones with hit acts, then don't waste your time. For radio, what you look like is obviously not important: it's what you sound like that counts, so there is no need to enclose photographs. For television, on the other hand, they are essential.

Make sure your name, address and telephone number are clearly marked on the cassette or record and biography. You cannot do this too many times. If your package gets split and the name is only on the biography, your unmarked tape or record will disappear into the huge pile of unusables in the corner. And having sent your material, do not expect to get a written reply; in fact, do not expect to get a reply at all. Including a stamped addressed envelope could encourage, though it will not ensure, the return of your tape.

One producer's view is that making demo tapes is only useful up to a point: 'It is far better for a new band to concentrate on doing gigs and establishing themselves. Anyone can do a demo tape nowadays. With the portable tape machines we get so many crappy cassettes. I am sympathetic to new bands trying to make it and don't want to discourage them, but some of them don't do themselves any favours. As for approaching companies direct – well, often people are more approachable than a band might think. But there is no short cut, no waiting-list. It all depends on making an impression.'

Use any contacts you possibly can. A word in the ear of a producer from a good friend, a respected manager, producer, lawyer, agent, local radio, music journalist – even an accountant – can make a world of difference. And remember that you will have to work with the media, too – the media as it is, not how you would like it to be. You have got to be visible. It's no good saying, for example, 'We're an album band, so we don't want to do a Saturday children's show.'

FORMING A BAND AND ESTABLISHING AN IMAGE

The biggest problem with bands is agreeing on major issues – where the band is heading, both musically and in terms of its image. Many new bands break up because one member starts heading off in a different direction from the one in which his group started out. It happens all the time. And the more members of the band, the more people there are to disagree. So keeping the band small is a good idea – it also means there's more money to go round on gigs.

Groups should be benign dictatorships. Democratic bands on the whole are no good: you need a leading light – for inspiration and for leadership.

Deciding what music to concentrate on in order to make the biggest impression can be another bone of contention. There is a difference between playing the sort of music you love and the type of music which will get you noticed.

One producer who is sent many tapes every week recommends a copycat approach: 'Music now is so imitative. The best thing to do is to work out which bands are successful and which big labels have stars of that kind. Then you can approach the labels which don't. Though there is a danger of that style falling out of fashion, it is still one way of going about things.

'Also you should be aware that pop music is very dance-oriented, now more than ever. Over half of the tapes sent in to me reflect no consciousness of that – which I find extraordinary. Rhythm is very important.

'Personally I look for some sign of individuality within the parameters of sounding like another, already-successful, sound. I need to be reassured that there is a good singer, the number is danceable and the band has a presentable image.'

You must be image-conscious. Although image is no longer more important than songs, we live in a world where images count for a great deal. A clear identity is essential. If Sigue Sigue Sputnik had had some good songs as well as an amazing visual appearance, they might have lasted longer than they did. You need to work yourselves out as a total package – music, style, appearance, what part of the musical spectrum you are aiming for – before starting to sell yourselves. To convince people, both those in the business *and* your public, you have to know where you are going. As one record company man puts it: 'The best bands have strategies, the worst just have talent.'

If you are too immersed in your music to be able to evaluate the rest of your presentation, then talk to someone you trust – a good friend or your manager – about your ideas. An outsider should be able to be objective, whereas you may have difficulty being so. Even a local journalist who has been following your career could be worth talking to.

One cynical view is that it is practically impossible to find 'real', innovative bands at the moment. Producers spend their time trying to produce more of the same sound, and the record company's view is that the market exists, therefore all it has to do is find the product – rather than the other way round.

NAMING THE GROUP

Try to come up with an original name. You will only store up problems if you become successful and then discover that your name has already been used.

The problem usually arises if you go to America. The name might have been OK for Britain, but if you suddenly find it has been used by an American band for several years that band will have the right to it. (The simplest way round this is to just put 'UK' after your name.)

If you take up a name by which another band is already widely recognized, that band can stop you using it. But if the same name is used by two unknown bands, the matter will rest on which one becomes well-known first.

MAKING A RECORD DEAL

Now that bands have rather more knowledge of the business – and past rip-offs – than they used to, and there are lawyers with specialized knowledge and experience, bands tend to get fairer deals with recording companies than was once the case. Performers are more likely to go into a deal knowing what to ask for and what terms to expect, and record companies are prepared to pay what they have to pay. Don't forget, there is a lot of competition for new talent nowadays. While it is important for the record company to be straight-talking, the band must be realistic, too, and recognize what it is up against. Honesty on both sides is vital.

Record companies have at least a dozen acts clamouring for their time. The more a band responds and co-operates, the better (this is even more the case in America, where record companies will give bands large sums of money yet do nothing until the band pesters them), but it is still crucial to know what the company has in mind.

Try to do a sensible deal, based on the assumption that you will achieve success. Weigh up the pros and cons: a large sum of money paid up front will mean a lower royalty rate, in all probability. Make sure the deal is workable. A new band should expect 10-12 per cent of the record's retail price, excluding VAT, scaling up to 14-15 per cent according to the quantity sold. An advance may be what you need and care about, but royalty percentages are important too.

Work out what you need with your manager. Bear in mind how much you need to live on, remembering you will have to put some money aside for tax and how much you need to equip the band. You must be honest with the record company, explaining exactly what the money is for. When you come to signing an agreement, you will probably get half immediately, a quarter when recording, and a quarter when you have finished recording.

A deal may sound generous but turn out not to be so when you work out what it actually has to pay for. Tears for Fears (a two-man band) recall one of their first deals: 'At the time we didn't take advice. We did deals which we thought were brilliant, but in fact we were getting half the amount we should have. We thought an advance of £10,000 was amazing, but we hadn't thought what it really meant. At that time in our lives, £10,000 seemed an enormous amount of money. But we didn't appreciate that it was meant to cover us for a year. In fact, it should have been £25,000.'

You need talent and you need luck, but you also need to

know the full implications of every step you take. Knowledge will at least help to minimize your chances of being ripped off.

One top manager offers this advice to new bands: 'Don't compromise your music. Be original. Pay attention to the business side of your career: you will regret it if you don't. Get a good lawyer. Remember that rock music is a business, but remember also that it's fun. Don't take it too seriously. Just follow your instincts. Be comfortable in what you are doing. And remember you will have to work hard. Rock is not a job, it's a lifestyle.'

Another manager sums up: 'It's a crazy business. In what other business can you go to someone, play them a tape of a band's ideas and ask for £100,000 – and the same again for promotion – when you can give no guarantee the record will sell, be written about or even played?'

CHAPTER 5

Playing live

There is an enormous difference between playing live and playing in the studio. Recording is cerebral, playing live is physical.

One singer describes it like this: 'When we perform live, it's new, very exciting. It's a quantum leap from the first construction of a song at home to performing in front of hundreds of people. It's marvellous, every time. It's mind-blowing.'

There are two reasons for playing live: to develop the band's ability and confidence as performers, and to give them feedback from the public – an unbiased reaction to their material and their way of performing.

John Blake of the *Daily Mirror* has strong views on gigging: 'I think bands *should* play live. It's good for their longevity. King and Marillion, for example, are hard-put to survive. It didn't matter so much a few years ago when studio bands were all the rage, but it does matter now. Frankie Goes to Hollywood were a very manufactured band, but when I saw them at Wembley Arena I was surprised how fantastically good they were live. If they hadn't been, they would never have been able to sustain a career.

'Playing live cuts out self-indulgence. A band may think they're brilliant and that one particular number is the one, but if they play live they'll get feedback, and when they see the reaction of an audience they might find another song goes down far better.

'Nothing around at the moment really excites me. It must be wide open for a band to really make it big. There's no competition – no Wham! or Duran Duran – the market is there for the taking. There's a real shortage of imagination at present.'

You need to keep playing live even when you have a

recording contract, to consolidate your fans' support. A record company might prefer you to put out album after album, which means spending all your time in the studio, rehearsing and recording, with no time for gigging. Touring does not sell quantities of records and that is what the record companies are primarily interested in – record sales. But playing live increases your credibility and hard-core following, so it is important to keep doing it.

If you feel strongly that you should be out on the road, say so. A good record company should be sympathetic to your wishes, if you can persuade it that this is best for you.

PRESENTATION

Rehearsal is all-important. You cannot rehearse enough. Playing music demands concentration, and thorough rehearsal will make you confident enough to project the music to the audience as effectively as possible without your having to worry about which chord comes next or where the riff comes. A shambolic set will do nothing for you.

Playing live also means projecting yourselves as performers, which needs as much thought and pre-planning as the music you play. Do you want to look scruffy, casual, smart or hip? Does the look fit with your music? Does it get what you are trying to say across to the audience? Once you have decided on the image you wish to put across, stick to it. As you build up a following your fans need to be able to lock into your image and believe in it. The image must look natural, so work on that.

Get to each gig as early as possible, equipped with spare strings, drum-sticks and so on, to give yourselves time to do a sound check. Make sure everyone in the band knows the order of the set.

While you're playing, you are bound to have the occasional problem. If you do have a disaster, keep going if you can. If not, wrap the number up and start another or finish the set and get off the stage quickly. If you do it well, the audience might not even realize what happened.

Lastly, enjoy yourselves. If you look like you're enjoying the gig, so will the audience. It's meant to be fun, after all.

GIGGING

In the old days, bands used to build their career by rehearsing, then playing live in pubs, then small clubs, then on the college circuit, large clubs and so on. It doesn't happen that way now. Everything depends on hit singles. You can play the Hammersmith Odeon without ever having played live before, simply as a result of recording success – like A-Ha, for example.

When the Housemartins first toured, before they had any hit singles, they had difficulty pulling in the crowds. Now, thanks to their hits, each gig is packed. Yet they sound the same now as they did in their pre-hit days.

'Studio' bands have been successful in the past, but even they have to play live in the end, so early experience can do nothing to harm any band's career.

When you are starting out it is essential to build up a following. Word-of-mouth is the most powerful form of publicity there is. Once a buzz has been created you will be able to interest local papers, music papers and eventually record companies, producers and other influential parties. And, of course, the bigger your following, the easier you'll find it to get the more important gigs.

Find a venue in your local area with which you can become identified. It need not necessarily be somewhere obviously associated with music, but could be a church hall, a scout hut – anywhere that is big enough to hold an audience, provided it conforms to current fire regulations (your gig will be shut down if it does not) and provided it has a music licence, or you obtain one yourself for the occasions in question. Try organizing a disco for part of the evening, after which you play live for an hour or so. You might get a bigger audience that way, and thus slowly build up your 'cult' following.

Even if you do it unpaid, the experience will be invaluable. You will have to keep going no matter what gaffes any of you makes during the performance, and you will get audience reaction to you and your material – especially important if you are trying out numbers you have written yourself. The experience of playing live will pay dividends when you come to make a demo tape and save on costly studio time. And if playing live and making the music business your career is what you want, making money from gigs should be a bonus, not an essential. Playing live sorts out the men from the boys: if you can't do it, then forget it.

Gone are the days of the 'sixties and 'seventies when we punters were happy to fork out £1 or so to listen to new bands. Then it seemed exciting, challenging, a good way to spend an evening. Now, we seem to prefer playing safe, only going to see known bands, and of course, we have many other ways of spending our leisure time. We think twice before paying £2 or more for a ticket to see an unknown act.

One group which knows the pub and college circuits well confirms this: 'People aren't going to pay to see an unknown band and it takes at least six months for any band to build up its own support. College students don't care who they see for a small entry fee, but they are very difficult to play to. You are competing with the disco, and if they don't like you they won't hang around.'

Out of London, the live scene is not so dire. One producer, based in the Thames Valley, comments: 'It's not that bad here. There must be about 500 local bands, with 200 working consistently. I think the interest in seeing live bands is on the increase. People are fed up with videos and "plastic" bands. A band needs to mean something when it plays now. All this interest in the oldies – the Beatles, Stones, Beach Boys, etc. – is just a sign of the times. The punters are not finding what they want in the music of the moment. Seeing bands play live, maybe in a sweaty pub, is new to them. It's exciting.'

Despite this view, overall the live scene has diminished over the last few years, and there are good reasons why. Discos are one of them: in many venues the seats have been removed so that people have room to dance – but they'll be dancing to recorded music, not a live band. Moreover, many of the places that *do* still cater for live performances care little for the punters, and would seem to be trying to discourage all but the most determined fans.

One journalist who has seen backstage of most venues

comments: 'Rock fans are treated like dirt. Wembley is disgusting: the conditions are appalling, the loos are filthy. Hammersmith Odeon is revolting, too. Many clubs are no better – they charge a lot for getting in and you get nothing in return. It's not like that in Paris, for example. The best club there is under a grass dome, is clean, and you have good views. And the backstage facilities are brilliant.'

Audiences expect much more than they used to from a live band. We are conditioned to seeing bands on videos, with high-quality, studio-produced sound, special effects and lighting, and we forget such quality cannot be reproduced on stage. This makes it especially hard for well-known bands, who are supposed to look and sound as impressive as they do on their videos. It also puts pressure on new bands to produce a more professional show than they may be capable of at that stage in their career.

Musicianship is important: sometimes bands forget this. Someone who has paid money to see you wants to have a good time. Listening to ten minutes of a self-indulgent track which you might well think brilliant is likely to leave your audience stone cold. That sort of behaviour is best kept to when you have a large following. If you can win over a crowd, you've got something going for you.

There is no doubt that the standard of many British bands playing live has fallen in recent years; some are truly appalling. Australian bands, on the other hand, are usually very good live and currently many of them are coming to Britain to establish themselves. The reason for this is that in Australia they have to play 200 gigs a year for three years before getting a record deal, so those that make it are highly experienced and good to watch. Let us hope some of their professionalism will rub off on UK bands.

As new groups proliferate, all trying to find places to play live, in a climate in which live venues are disappearing, the situation cannot easily improve. More bands, fewer venues, means more hassle – and more power to the agent or booker!

The trick is hassling, or the art of gentle persuasion. If you want to gig in London, for example, go through *Time Out* or the music press for gig listings. Check out the venues, find out whom to approach and ring them. Send them a tape – clearly marked with your name and address – and a picture if you have one, and then start exerting pressure. If you have any contacts, use them. Most clubs have to be approached through their booker. A lot use agents, but if you approach direct with a professional attitude, you might have a chance. 'Professional' means sending in well-presented tapes and photos and making a personal visit. The easiest way is to get in with a publican who will put you on as a support, or to get in with a headlining band.

The Mean Fiddler in Harlesden High Street is one place you can easily approach direct. Its booker will listen to you, your tape or video if you ring, write or pop in. This venue has 'new band' nights at the beginning of the week and if you can bring 100 people into the club it won't cost you anything. You might even make money.

There's no charge for PA, lighting or an engineer, but you do have to put down a £50 deposit against the 100 attendances. You will be given tickets which you can sell or give away as you wish. If 100 people attend, you get your deposit back, and if the club likes you, you should get a chance to play a support later on.

The Marquee, in London W1, on the other hand, deals only with agents, with the odd exception for groups that have a huge following. A club such as the Town & Country Club (Kilburn High Road) occasionally has showcase nights, but these will be taken by promoters with a batch of new bands. If you look in the music papers and see who is promoting groups similar to yours, you could try ringing that promoter. Very occasionally the Town & Country Club will promote an evening itself, but only using bands already known to the venue. Any tapes sent in unsolicited are normally sent back.

A university such as Brunel in Uxbridge usually books acts through established agencies, but may promote some groups direct. A support band would get £50 and free use of PA and lights. And because it can't offer local bands many support gigs, Brunel University sometimes hires out the venue and lets the bands promote themselves. This would cost about £275 for the hall, with the PA and publicity to pay for on top.

So do your homework before approaching the venue.

One seasoned keyboards-player who knows the gigging scene well explains: 'There are fewer places in the suburbs which are interested in new music, but lots of places which will take new bands as long as they do covers of well-known songs. London is less difficult in this respect, but it's much more of a problem to get bookings in the capital.

'The Greyhound [Fulham Palace Road], for example, used to be a rough old dive. [This is no longer the case.] Anyone could get a gig if they waited long enough. Nowadays, bands have to have a single out – or to be able to con the bookers into thinking they will be the next band to make it big. Then they *might* get a support gig, if they're lucky.'

Even small gig venues are difficult to find. Not long ago a band could play for nine months in England without playing the same gig twice. Now it would be hard pushed not to play the same venue twice in one month.

An actively gigging band should aim to work about two or three times a month, which is a good average for a band promoting its own material. It should aim to spend a month working every week, then have a break for rehearsing or writing new songs. Gigging has become very expensive for bands; they can expect to make little or nothing out of it – if indeed the cost of travel and hiring equipment do not put them out of pocket. Four to nine years ago it cost £100 a night to hire the gear you needed for a gig, including a roadie, a van, etc. Now it can set you back at least £400.

In London, where you really need to gig if you are hoping to attract the attention of record companies, you are unlikely to make much, if anything, out of a pub or small club gig, but on the other hand many London gigs now provide house PAs and lighting. Clubs certainly will and pubs might. But they need to be checked out – if the PA is too ropey you might as well not bother, especially if you are hoping for someone who matters to come and listen to the band. Presentation and first impressions are all-important.

If you are supporting a band that is further up the ladder than you, it will have its own PA, and you will be expected to pay something towards it. Such considerations need to be worked out in advance.

Hardly any London pubs pay a fee nowadays; usually the deal is that the performers take a percentage of the door money. Some places will give the band the entire door takings – they make money on drink sales. They might demand a percentage of the door for use of their PA, or advertising, printing of tickets, etc., if they provide any of this. If there is a house PA the pub should provide an engineer. It is also up to you, the band, to rally people round – and not to give too many free tickets away. But weigh up the odds – you may consider the live experience is worth more than making a few pounds. And next time you could try getting together with another band to fill a gig.

Outside London you could expect to earn a little from a pub date – especially if you attract a big audience. But the ratio of groups to venues is now so high that venues need not always pay for their live entertainment. They usually pay for the headlining band, but little or nothing for support bands. Way back in 1964 you could get £150 even if you were tenth in line: now you would receive nothing.

The college circuit has also tailed off, mainly owing to lack of funds and also because of competition from discos. Colleges rarely have a PA, so that is one expense to bear in mind, but if you can get a gig they do pay money.

Good places to play in London (at the time of writing) are Dingwall's, the Town & Country Club, the Marquee, the Rock Garden, the Mean Fiddler, the Fulham Greyhound, Fulham King's Head, Greenwich Tunnel Club, Putney Half Moon, Herne Hill Half Moon, the Croydon Cartoon, the Limelight, Le Beatroute and the 100 Club.

Colleges such as Brunel University, Uxbridge, North Staffordshire Poly (Stafford), Buckingham College of Higher Education, Oxford Poly, Loughborough University, the Manchester Union and the Roehampton Institute for Girls are all using live bands. They are also hard gigs to play. The students expect to be entertained and won't put up with amateurishness.

Most venues in London have showcase nights for new bands, but the policy is often for the group to bring its fans with it. They have to guarantee, say, two coachloads, or the equivalent entry-fee money. It is up to the band whether it charges its fans or pays itself.

Although many clubs book only through agents, if you approach them in the right way and your tape is really good, you might be able to talk your way into a support gig.

The sort of sums you can expect in London are as follows. A small venue such as the Cricketers (Oval) will pay £50-£200. Playing at the Clarendon, London W6, where tickets cost £3.50-£4.50, the headline group might get £200. At Hammersmith Odeon tickets cost from £5 upwards, and you could get paid £1000-£1500; at the Town & Country Club, which seats 1200-1300 people, you could receive £1000-£3000; to play Wembley Stadium, with tickets costing £8 upwards, might mean as much as £10,000.

TOURING

Touring is exhausting – no doubt about it. There used to be an element of glamour in going abroad, but travelling is so commonplace nowadays that that has gone. And even though you may be lucky enough to tour abroad, you're unlikely to see much of the country you're visiting. Usually you just play the gig, fall into bed, get up early, sit in the van and hurtle hundreds of miles to the next gig, and so on. Even touring round England can be totally chaotic. It needs a good deal of organization to arrange the gigs in an order that makes logistical sense: it's all too easy to find yourself in the north of England one night, down south the next and back up north the following one.

But for many bands the joy of performing live is worth all the aggro incurred in touring. One band interviewed for this book said they would go mad if they couldn't tour, though doing so makes little sense for them economically: 'We try to break even, but it is very difficult. You need reasonable lighting, gear and hotel accommodation, so the band is not exhausted. Fees are hardly ever enough to cover costs. But record companies do like a band to tour.

'Playing live is like making a base. It gets you more press

and increases your following. So you build up a hard core who will always buy your records.'

Touring can be fun, but it is hard work and can take quite a toll on your personal life, health and sanity; bands often break up after tours. This was one band's experience: 'We did a disastrous three-week tour round Germany, just the five of us, in two Sherpa vans, humping 2-kilowatt amps around, all the instruments (we had no roadies or help) and driving eight hours at a time with three of us squashed in front. Once was enough!'

Anne Nightingale, who has accompanied several bands on tour, comments: 'An artist's personal life is difficult when touring, especially if he has to leave a partner behind. You must be mentally and emotionally strong. You have to take hard knocks, both physically and mentally. There are so many pressures. A solid home life really makes a difference. Stars often come from either a very secure family background or an appalling one. I've seen how exhausting it is touring with Police.'

Touring nearly broke up Tears for Fears. Curt Smith recalls: 'Last year we did an eight-month tour around the world . . . It was a tremendous strain on my relationship with Roland [Orzabal]. We weren't used to living out of each other's pockets.

'It was so bad at one time we nearly broke up. I was on my way to New York to fly home. Paul King, our manager, met me at the airport. He didn't do the "What do you think you're doing?" routine. He just talked to me, saying, "Don't make a rash decision. This is *your career*." He persuaded me to go back for a couple of weeks, and it turned out all right. I learnt then you mustn't make a quick decision – it's so easy to make the wrong one in the heat of the moment.

'Now Roland and I are closer than ever. I think every group has to go through this once, and if you have determination to keep going it strengthens you and makes you better.'

Financially, the rewards for touring are poor (especially if your manager is taking a percentage of your gross earnings), as for gigging, while the expenses are greater.

There's certainly little money in touring when you start. Touring outside England can be more profitable, however: there is a much bigger market in Europe, and America, too, can bring high rewards.

Because touring is so expensive you should ideally be signed to a record company, or possibly a publisher, before you undertake it. A band would never have the resources to fund its own tours. A record company does, although it will expect the cost will be recouped – in part or in full – from future royalties.

Major acts need to play to 6000 people a day on tour to break even. A smaller band should start making a small profit playing to about 2000 people.

Ed Bicknell, Dire Straits' manager, revealed that the band 'loses £30,000 a day in England. But they make money everywhere else. New Zealand is especially good.'

On a club tour, you will probably do about 10-12 dates. Then, as you meet more and more people, you will go into secondary towns. Playing in fewer but larger venues is obviously better. You won't start making money until you are playing to 1500-2000 people.

It is vital to break in the USA. The US still counts for 60 per cent of the world market for overall music earnings. Britain may have the kudos, but America provides the hard cash. As a new group you can tour the USA on a shoestring – if, for example, you all muck in and travel in a hired bus. There are more chances of getting a support tour there, too.

If you just like gigging and don't care too much what sort of place you work in, or want a break from everything else, there are lots of tacky places where American bands won't play, but English groups can – without losing money. For example, Furniture and Sector 27 both made money in America. And with the help of a video you can get known first, so you are touring as a known band – although you have never played in the country before.

The simplest and easiest way to start touring is to buy into someone else's tour. The cost for buying into a major UK tour at present ranges from £2000 to £10,000; £5000 is about the norm.

Don't think you will be paid for supporting a star band.

Sometimes you will get a paltry £100; mostly you will have to pay the headlining band. Psychedelic Furs received £15,000 from one of their support bands, but that was unusually high.

So many bands want to tour and find it difficult to arrange that it is not surprising this custom has arisen. And it is not totally unfair. By supporting a known band you are more likely to get attention from the media, and be seen by a large number of rock fans – although it is possible they will turn up only for the starring act. When the Young Ones were supporting the Boomtown Rats, for example, they managed to build up such a following in one area that at times they were getting a better reaction than the Rats. But they would never have been able to do that if they had been touring on their own.

CHAPTER 6

Record companies

The main objective of record companies is to sell records, so one of the most important departments of any record company is its A & R (artists and repertoire) department, which has the task of finding the groups and solo artists who can produce a saleable sound. Once it has found a new group it believes is special, it will aim to build it to star status. At that time, and probably a little before, both parties – record company and artists – should start raking in the money: more for the company than for the artists, admittedly, but as long as you have been careful about having your contract checked out, you should see a fair amount coming your way too.

It must be remembered that record companies are businesses, first and foremost. They are not there just for the love of it. What is more, for every successful group they handle there are likely to be ten costly failures. Your success will pay for those failures, and *vice versa*.

There are basically two types of record company in Britain. The major companies – the largest of which are EMI, CBS, WEA, RCA Ariola and PolyGram (Polydor, Phonogram and London); and the independents, of which the major companies are Chrysalis, Island, Virgin and A & M; smaller but well-established labels include Mute, Beggars' Banquet, Rough Trade, ZTT and Cherry Red; there are also a host of tiny, struggling companies which come and go with regularity.

In all there are about 600 small record labels in Britain at present, only 20-25 of which may be considered 'serious' independent companies.

A major record company is usually divided into four parts – one which deals with recording and releasing records, one with acquisition of repertoire, one with manufacturing (pressing plants, sleeves, labels, etc.), and one with distribution (which holds stocks and shifts the product into the shops). The sales force is sometimes part of the distribution side, sometimes part of the recording side.

It is extremely expensive to run a distribution company, which is why many independent record labels are distributed by major record companies. The smaller independents who do not have the pressing, distribution or marketing facilities of the bigger companies use outside specialist companies for these functions, or that specific arm of a major company.

The smaller independents cannot take a group on to the international big-time as its career develops, because it does not have the infrastructure to cope with this. It could be said that the independents currently act as unpaid A & R departments to the majors. The independents are the ones who take the risks, and are generally interested in the less obviously commercial music. The other risk-takers, who are becoming more prominent on the music scene, are the independent producers (see Chapter 9).

As one independent producer puts it: 'Major record companies are undergoing a change. They are becoming more like the American ones – just huge distribution and marketing companies rather than finders and developers. Ten to fifteen years ago people like us were employed by a record company. I was.

'Record companies have lost the ability to put bands on the road, to build them from nothing and stick with them through the first two or three years.'

The 'indies' and the production companies do the hard work – finding and working on the new group, building its reputation; the majors jump in when the group is just starting to make it, pump the money in and wait for their stars to be born.

Some independents are quite happy for this to happen. Ian McNay, managing director of Cherry Red, says: 'Majors often approach us waving cheque books, but that is OK with us. We keep the publishing and take a percentage of the recording contract: that way we keep an involvement with the group we started.

'Our strength is through the press. We know who likes what, we send each record to good people who will do a review and a feature. That sells records. We also get plays on *Peel* and *Janice Long*. We very rarely get daytime play, though it all depends on the sort of record.

'We will take an act and build a base sale through the image of our label, with reviews and late-night plays. Some groups, the Girl, for instance, grow slowly. They took four to five years. Now they are selling gold and silver.

'Some bands gig. They work live all over the world rather than be on the dole. They are making a living and most importantly they are enjoying it. No bands with us are rich, but being with us gives them an opportunity to make a record.'

Meo Thompson of Rough Trade puts it like this: 'The difference between us and the majors is that we are more informal, there is more personal contact and we are not committed to see the market go on whatever – we are prepared to break out. Also in a major there will be competition for attention *inside* the company, let alone outside.

'It is important for a record company to be straight-talking. Honesty is vital. And the band has to be realistic, to know what it is up against.'

Indies are generally good at initial sales – getting the first 3-4000 copies sold, building local interest. You will not get the money you might from a major, but you might well find an attitude that you prefer when starting out. And money is not everything. A huge advance does not guarantee you an instant hit. Very often creative flair and the ability and willingness to build your credibility slowly are far more important. However, eventually money will be needed if you are to break not only in Great Britain, but Europe, America and the rest of the world, which is where the big money is to be made.

The large independents can, theoretically, offer the best of both worlds – the personal approach combined with the power. In practice, too, this is often the case. However, each company takes on only four to ten new groups a year, so not every group can go with its ideal record company.

One major's view on indies is that 'independents are good for development. The live scene used to be the breeding ground for groups; now, indies have taken over. That's a very healthy situation. It gives bands somewhere to start.'

Another advantage of an independent company – if you are not looking for an enormous advance and long-term involvement – is that they do not usually want to tie you down for as long as a major would.

Martin Mills of Beggars' Banquet says: 'We don't tend to sign immediate overnight-success pop bands. It could take two years building the band, during which time we might spend £100,000. We prefer it that way.

'Many of the bands with BB started by doing a one-off album. We don't ask them to mortgage their future. Hopefully they will get on and stay with us. Most bands end up signing for five years and a chunk of money.

'We don't lose a lot to majors. We are in the ideal situation: we can combine the personal approach of an indi and the muscle of a major. We put out fewer bands now and concentrate on them more.'

When choosing which record company to sign to – provided you have a choice, which will not necessarily be the case – it is important to find one you feel happy with. Take the time to go round the company. Does it have an atmosphere you can respond to? Is its attitude the one you are looking for? Find out how quickly it wants tangible success. Will you be dropped if your first record doesn't make the charts? Does it want to build you slowly? Will it treat you as you want to be treated?

It is no good signing with a company for a big advance if you are unhappy with the way it is intending to develop your career. You will only be unhappy and discontented, and have to spend valuable time arguing instead of working with the company for your mutual benefit. The same applies in reverse, of course. One record company managing director admits to pretty strong feelings about bands' attitudes to record companies: 'It gets my goat. There tends to be a "them and us" attitude on the part of many bands. They come in with the view that the record company is out to screw them up and screw them out of money, so there is great distrust between the two parties right from the outset.

'It's a great shame. Workers and bosses should be able to work together. Cliff Richard has been with the same company [EMI] throughout his career thanks to trust and respect.'

An A & R man comments: 'You have got to remember that there's no point a record company ripping a band off or upsetting a group. If they are unhappy, or there is not enough money, it's no good – they won't work or record as well as they could. You want a deal that works – one that is advantageous to both sides.'

The major companies are interested in commercial music, into which they are prepared to pump thousands of pounds (£150,000 for the first year is quite normal for a newly signed band) and expect to make hundreds of thousands of pounds back. Singles very rarely make money: they are the loss leader for the albums. That is where the money is.

The advantage of the major companies is that they have the money, structure and influence to turn stars into megastars. They have an established worldwide operation and can pour money into a growing group. The smaller independents, on the other hand, will deal with you on a more personal basis; they are less regimentalized and have the enthusiasm, time and inclination to build a band gradually.

The majors no longer have the time to devote their energy to shaping and building a new band. Rob Dickins, managing director of WEA, says: 'We like acts in a completely packaged form. We are not prepared to do much work on a group.' And his is not the only major company with such a policy. Carol Wilson of Phonogram admits: 'A big record company can't do all the individual jobs, so the more groups do for themselves the better. It also proves they are serious and keen.'

One independent company says of the majors: 'A major company shows interest in one group in ten or fifteen of those it has signed – so you have to be lucky. It can be just like a sausage machine. The company has to keep putting out records – you can't have A & R and production departments not doing anything – so they put out dross. By sheer statistics you have a far better chance of happening with an indi.'

This is perhaps an extreme view of the situation and is not the case with every major. They certainly *used* to have the time and energy to devote to new bands; some still do, and if they have any sense all will start doing so again. Older stars may be holding their own at the moment, but a regular influx of new bands who will become tomorrow's stars are the lifeblood of any record company.

David Munns, who was until recently A & R director of EMI, explains his policy: 'We will take a band in any stage of development. We are sometimes interested more in the artist than in the song, but bands who want to develop on their own with little interference from record companies should go to independents.'

Jonathan King, who has been in the business for many years, as entrepreneur, songwriter and at one time performer, feels strongly that major record companies should be doing their own groundwork. As he puts it: 'Record companies should be more like baseball teams, and have "farm clubs" where they start with small bands and work on them.'

On the whole a major record company will try to take your career into the fast lane. If it pumps a lot of money into you, it will want as quick a return as possible, and that means high-profile publicity, advertising, touring and public appearances. If you want to take things a little more slowly, give yourself time to develop and have less pressure on you to do things you do not really want to do, then an independent company will be more suitable.

Clive Banks, managing director of Island Records, admits: 'I often spend time trying to slow groups down. We say, "We like you but no singles this year – we'll just help you to build." Some groups don't understand that.'

This view is echoed many times over in the industry. One A & R man says: 'I would sooner it happened naturally and quietly. Now managers make the buzz, the record companies fuel it – rather than it happening slowly. We will spend the same money on a new group over two years as on a more established group in nine months. It is just a slower process. As long as we can see progress and the band's career is building it justifies the expense.'

Roy Eldridge, managing director of Chrysalis, agrees: 'I like to take a group as naturally as we can. If you try to force success, it doesn't last. The speed at which it works depends on many circumstances, including a lot of luck. The Housemartins, for example, happened very quickly. Go West won a BPI [British Phonographic Industry] award when very new.'

With huge amounts of money being spent on a new group, they can be pushed very quickly into the public eye, but this often means that groups face harsh criticism as well as praise. The sudden attention can be hard to get used to, and living up to the hype can prove to be quite a test of nerves and stamina for any artist.

For someone who has never been a professional anything before, just playing in a back room and doing a few local gigs, the pressure can be unbearable. This is why so many groups have one hit and just disappear: being dumped straight into the deep end means you either sink or swim.

A & R DEPARTMENTS

A & R (artists and repertoire) departments are not large. They are generally made up of an A & R director with a small team under him. The more active A & R departments will have one person who spends most of his or her time at the back of clubs and pubs, seeking out new bands in their infancy.

The junior is the talent scout whose job it is to sift through the daily influx of demo tapes. Any solicited tapes will go direct to the person for which they are intended; unsolicited tapes go to the scout, who may or may not have the knowledge, ability and experience to make an objective appraisal of what he hears.

So it is a rather sad fact that your tape could well be heard only by someone who has little experience in the business and will recommend or discard your tape purely on his own personal feelings rather than from a position of objectivity. This is one reason why unsolicited tapes rarely get anywhere, let alone listened to by the head of the A & R department. All A & R departments are bombarded with tapes, letters and phone calls from hopeful bands. They have far too many to handle, let alone reply to individually. Although some A & R departments do profess to send some sort of reply to bands, many do not, and few ever return tapes.

Simon Draper of Virgin explains: 'A group has to understand that A & R men are inundated with requests from bands who want to be heard and seen.

'And remember that the investment a record company needs to make, if taking a serious, long-term, worldwide view, is huge. It is not something undertaken lightly. Often the decision is based on a hunch. Belief and commitment in a band are vital if a company is to pick you out of the thousands of hopefuls.'

A & R departments say they are looking for originality, intelligent, well-written songs and charisma, and for artists with a quality that will last. Unfortunately at the moment they are also looking for similarity, recognizability and a sound that fits into a familiar successful pattern. There is not much call for challenging, out-of-the-ordinary music. A & R people have too much to lose to stick their necks out a long way.

Punk had an immeasurable influence on the music business, opening it up enormously. If it had not been for the Sex Pistols *et al* the music scene would be even more backward-looking than it has become. But punk is now dead and innovation seems to have been put into the pending file for the time being.

One A & R director says: 'We look for a natural songwriting talent which will endure – also for character, and for a "proper artist", someone who will transcend fashion, like a Sting or a Ray Charles of the future.

'An artist must have the ability to reach an audience. Sometimes you get a really good songwriter and musician who has the character of an empty yoghurt carton.'

Derek Green of China says he looks for 'style, not necessarily brilliant ability. I listen to the music first, then meet the manager. From there I go on to get an impression of the group – their attitude, how smart they are, their commitment. I am looking for an act capable of growing talent-wise.

'A lot comes down to how much a gambler you are. It's a bit like being a horse-trainer: you shorten the odds because you know something about horse flesh, but in the end you can never guarantee a win.'

Another A & R director of a major company comments in much the same vein: 'I look for how they sell an act, good looks, two or three hit singles on the demo tape. I need to hear a good song with possibilities. It doesn't have to be proficient. When I look at a group's music, I am looking for albums.

'I have never signed a group just from a cold tape. We get recommendations from a network of people – agents, shop managers, bookers, etc. For example, Sting was recommended to me by a Virgin shop manager in Newcastle.'

Another director of a major record company looks for complete dedication: 'I have to believe in a band's talent, then I have to believe they are as committed as I am. We don't operate a mud-against-the-wall policy. Each band must count. We have to be confident they will work and want to make it.'

One point all record companies agree upon is that they never – or very, very rarely – sign groups from an unsolicited tape. In their view, if the group does not have a recommendation it is not worth a recommendation: in other words, it is not good enough or is at too early a stage of its career. To have a recommendation means you are competent, serious, know what you are doing and are therefore worth looking at.

Most record companies hope to sign a band for as long as possible, and some hope it will be forever. As one spokesman says: 'We don't offer a fortune, just a living wage. I will talk for hours with groups before and after signing. It can take a long time for groups to feel befriended and understood. I am prepared to give them that time.

'Our attitude is not just about signing to put out singles and forgetting it if they don't work. We are not into marketing instant smash hits. I like to build a band slowly. We might put a band out live for a year, which can cost as much as doing one single.'

WHERE THE MONEY GOES

It is much harder for a record company to launch a single today than it used to be, owing to the rising costs and the necessity for a video. In addition to that you need pictures, tour support, advertising and merchandising, which together can cost from £50,000 to £150,000.

One director of a major company reckons you can make an album for £10,000 with a new band, but that amount would not be acceptable for an international album. Nor would it include the cost of a video. He says: 'If you make an album for £150,000 and it *does* break, the album will be ready to go everywhere. It is easy to spend £200,000-£500,000.'

Another reason for bands costing record companies more money is because there are so few around that are any good. When something really impressive comes up all the record companies try to sign the band, and the price goes up. This always happens during periods when real talent is thin on the ground.

If you sign with a record company, you might be offered, say, a 12 per cent royalty on the retail price of each record. You might well wonder where the other 88 per cent goes. On an album a record company hopes to make a 5 per cent profit, but on a single there is usually a loss. Distribution costs account for about 25 per cent of the cost, manufacture (pressing), advertising and promotion about 15 per cent each, design and packaging account for the rest. For example, on a 7-inch single retailing at £1.49:

Trade price	£1.04
Distribution	.26
Pressing	.16
Advertising and promotion (including plugging)	.16
Design and packaging	.08
Artist's royalties	.18
Mechanical royalties	.08
A & R	.08

= £1.00, which leaves a pre-tax profit of £0.04, before overheads.

On an album retailing at £6 the cost would be:

Trade price	£3.45
Distribution	.86
Pressing	.35
Advertising and promotion	.30
Design and packaging	.20
Artist's royalties	.65
Mechanical royalties	.30
A & R	.22

Discounting overheads that leaves a pre-tax profit of 57p.

CHAPTER 7

Publishing

The idea of paying for the right to play somebody else's music is said to have started in a Parisian café at some time in the dim and distant past when a group of composers heard their music being played and refused to pay for their meal until they had been paid for their work.

Musical works have been bought and sold in the Western world ever since the Church ceased to be the primary employer of musicians, and probably before then. Until 1842, the date of the first Copyright Act covering musical composition, there was no protection at all for writers of musical works. Any musician could perform anyone else's musical works in public without paying a royalty. But that first Act, in its infancy, did little to help composers because it was virtually impossible to enforce.

Two further Acts in 1902 and 1906 allowed for infringements to be dealt with summarily and for the first time composers were able to earn an income from their compositions. But until 1914 publishers did not receive royalties from the public performance of works other than dramatic or stage works. Instead they relied on concert performances, which not only provided box-office income but increased sheet music sales.

Sheet music remained the main source of income for composers and songwriters until the 1920s. Although Edison's first phonograph was on sale in 1877, double-sided discs did not come on to the market until 1905, and slowly mechanical royalties (monies paid out of record sales to composers or songwriters) as a form of income took over from sheet sales. As 'light' music became increasingly popular, income from records became more and more important. After the First World War owning a gramophone became more common: though expensive, they were no longer regarded as eccentricities.

Len Thorpe, managing director of Chappell Music, one of the biggest publishing companies in Britain, with a catalogue of over 50,000 songs, explains: 'The whole premise of publishing has changed dramatically over the years, with the invention of the gramophone and then TV and radio. Income from these – copyright fees and mechanical royalties – gradually became much more important than that generated by sheet music.

'We used to sell 100,000 shilling [5p] copies of a song. Now we'll sell 10,000 or fewer, even if the song reaches no.1. Another difference is that everyone used to have a piano in their house, which someone could play. Now, other forms of entertainment take precedence.

'The main source of sheet income today is from compilations. But there are only three active printers of popular sheet music left. Most top twenty numbers will be available on sheet music, depending on the type of record. If you have a lot of men shouting over amplifiers, it is impossible to transcribe. The same thing applies to weird modern music. Half of it cannot be transcribed, let alone played from a score.'

Nowadays publishing has widened its tentacles to cover not only records, cassettes and CDs, cinemas, theatres, all performances in public places, but video, cable and satellite outlets. By the year 2000 publishers could be controlling performances on the moon!

The possibilities of wider and wider usage of music are in fact creating problems for publishers. The Music Publishers' Association is very concerned about the situation: 'We are looking for a united industry,' says a spokesman, 'but there are many problems now with the new technology. How can a UK publisher know what royalties to pick up when, say, a person in California has a satellite dish which picks up 100 different stations?

'There is a feeling that in twenty years' time copyright could go out of the window. Also in the future there could be a central computer enabling anyone who wanted sheet music to ask for it and have the piece printed out' on his own computer – which would make copyright impossible to control by current methods.

As record companies are primarily concerned with recording and selling records, publishers have to look after all uses of the music recorded – musical scores (printed music), video, television, radio, lyrics in books and magazines, live performance and so on. They are the controllers of music product. If a publisher does his job properly, he makes sure music is exploited to the full and that maximum royalties are achieved.

But publishers have become lazy; they have sometimes been described as acting more like bankers, merely collecting and distributing royalties from home and abroad. Groups approach them with a song that has been written, performed and recorded. All they want from a publisher is a means of registering copyright, and an administrator.

The publisher's duties also include policing, registering songs correctly with PRS, and dealing with overseas business relating to the music in question. The composer/songwriter needs international interest if he/she is to make money.

A good publisher will also act as nursemaid and financial adviser, and give his clients access to the company's copyright and legal departments.

As one publisher puts it: 'Publishing takes the aggro from the writer. It is like selling a house. You employ estate agents to do the dirty work for you. Likewise you employ a publisher to look after the rights of the songs for you. In the old days publishers would take a song from a writer and look after his sheet-music interests. In the last ten to fifteen years, they have concentrated on getting the song recorded. We only print works automatically if they reach the top ten; sometimes we print them if they reach the top twenty.'

With more and more singer/songwriters forming their own publishing companies – which if done with good contacts and the right advice will reap far higher financial benefits than signing away a third or more of your income to another organization – publishers have started to work for their money again, although they are no longer able to demand 50 per cent of the writer's income. This used to be the norm; now it is far more usual to have a 60/40 or 70/30 percentage split – in the writer's favour.

Publishers are the custodians of the copyright of musical works. The writer is the prime owner of his work; he assigns his rights in that work to the publisher for a certain period of time. The publisher takes a percentage of all income earned from that material and to earn his cut the publisher undertakes to exploit that material as best he can.

But some do little to realize the value of the songs assigned to them. There have been many cases of publishers sending indiscriminate piles of songs to record companies and artists, thereby wasting everybody's time. A good publisher must know what sort of song a record company or artist is looking for, and by sending only the right type of work will not only be more likely to have it accepted but also encourage recording companies or artists to come to him.

It follows that a small, efficient publisher who knows his business and is prepared to work hard for you is often better than a huge corporation which has a good bank of well-known writers keeping its coffers full and thus lessening the necessity for it to promote its lesser-known writers. On the other hand a large publisher will have well-established access to foreign royalties – which can easily count for more than UK ones.

As a writer/performer you will therefore be faced with another decision: whether to go for a major publisher who has the pull and the power or an independent publisher who is likely to take a more personal interest in your work and have more time to concentrate on making it earn money for you.

A publishing company has to collect every penny from all over the world to earn its cut properly. Everyone trusts a good company to do that, but a smaller one might not be so efficient. Publishing has become very competitive, especially in the UK.

Independent publishers tend to have smaller staff, be more approachable and have more time for new bands. They will often take a band on before it is signed by a record company.

One independent publisher describes his approach as follows: 'New bands are great to work with. They have desire, enthusiasm. I picked up one group before they got a record deal because a producer who was an old mate told me about them. I went up to Glasgow and saw them at rehearsal. I liked all their songs and heard two singles – which is unusual (normally you only hear two or three good songs). They looked the part and handled themselves well. I signed them, gave them a token £1000, for goodwill, and a 60/40 deal. I put them in a studio to do a demo tape and then RCA gave them a recording deal.'

You can either sign a publishing agreement for one specific song, or, more likely if you are starting out, an agreement for all songs you may write over a specified period of years. You should receive an advance from a publisher, the amount depending on your status and on whether or not you have a record deal. In the past publishers used to pay their writers a small retainer, but this is no longer standard practice.

If you do have a recording deal you should receive a better advance because the publisher knows he will be receiving royalties from recordings of your material that are sold and played, and a more advantageous royalty cut, e.g. 70/30 rather than 60/40.

But if you are finding it difficult to get a recording deal then a publishing deal could tide you over with the advance and, possibly, royalties from covers (recordings of your material made by others) and the publisher – if he is any good – should endeavour to obtain a record deal for you. If he does, you should receive a further advance.

It used to be unheard of for a publisher to sign a group before it had a record deal. Publishers never went out to see new bands. But as Peter Reichardt of Warner's explains: 'When punk started, I and Rob Dickins [now managing director of WEA] started to go and see bands, and we picked up the Sex Pistols. Because we got them early, there was much more money in it for us.'

An artist's publishing is an important source of income and some smaller record companies will only sign performers if they can have the publishing as well. Major record companies usually have their own publishing arm, but do not generally insist on having both recording and publishing if the artist wishes to go elsewhere.

In some cases a publishing company will do far more than a record company to promote a song. It may have licensing deals abroad and be able to get more publicity and therefore more sales than the record company is interested in doing – or has time to do.

For example, a major record company with many artists on its books can become disenchanted with one record if a hotter one comes along. In such a case the publisher may have to take over all the work of promotion. There is sometimes close co-operation between the publisher and record company in the choice of songs to be recorded. On the other hand you may find your A & R people are prima donnas who want their own choice of song and don't want the publisher's opinion.

Publishing is still big business. If you write a hit record, you and your publisher will go on earning for years.

One singer/songwriter who left the business several years ago to join a religious sect was reported to have received a half-yearly royalty cheque for £90,000 recently. Some standard songs, like 'White Christmas', are recorded yearly; 'I Left My Heart in San Francisco' and 'Angel Eyes' have each been recorded by over 40 artists. There is also huge money to be made from the use of songs in television series and advertising campaigns. 'Nellie the Elephant', a 1957 hit, is currently being used in a television series for a fee of £20,000-plus, and the re-releases of such elderly recordings as Percy Sledge's 'When a Man Loves a Woman' and Ben E. King's 'Stand by Me' have earned a small fortune for the songs' writers. 'Try a Little Tenderness', a hit from way back in 1932, is another song that found new popularity as a result of an advertising campaign. Even the dreadful 'Chicken Song' put out by the Spitting Image team earned the songwriters about £50,000.

According to the Performing Right Society gross revenue in 1986 from all sources (including radio, television and live performance) was £85.2 million, made up of £54.2 million from Great Britain and Ireland; £27 million from overseas territories; and £4 million investment income. Out of these monies £69.4 million, the sum available after administration costs and tax, was distributed to members – songwriters, composers and publishers.

A further breakdown, expressed in percentage terms, reveals that 39 per cent of the income came from British and Irish radio and TV; 31½ per cent from overseas; 25 per cent from British and Irish performance, and 4½ per cent from investment income. The bulk of the overseas royalties came from North America, followed closely by Western Europe. Australasia provides the third-largest income, then Africa and the Middle East. The lowest income comes from the Soviet Union, Eastern Europe, and Central and South America.

The revenue was distributed as follows: 40¼ per cent went to writer members, 26 per cent to publisher members, 15 per cent to foreign affiliated societies; 18 per cent was devoted to administration, ½ per cent was used for donations and ¼ per cent retained in reserves. (These figures are further broken down in the relevant *Performing Right Yearbook*.)

This, of course, is only part of the royalties that may be earned from the ownership of copyright of a piece of music. Monies for mechanical royalties (collected by MCPS, the Mechanical Copyright Protection Society) can also provide a good revenue.

As a minor writer this money will be an extra bonus to your earnings. Only the top few writers earn enough money from royalties to live on.

CHAPTER 8

Managers

A manager has to be many things – a psychologist, a businessman, accountant, lawyer and diplomat. It helps if he is also personable, far-thinking and streetwise. If he has contacts, power and money, so much the better.

Yet signing with a successful manager who is handling a major star is not necessarily the best course of action for a new artist or group. He may be able to pull deals because of his star client – with record companies, agents, and so on – and pay for you to fly round the world, but what happens when meetings are postponed because the star takes and demands priority, or you suddenly find your manager is out of the country for eleven months of the year touring with his other client?

It can be difficult to know how to avoid the managers who will take advantage of you and find one who will take you to stardom. There have been many cases catalogued of managers who have orchestrated large-scale rip-offs. The Sex Pistols and David Bowie lost considerable amounts. Paul McCartney, Pete Townshend, Joan Armatrading and Ray Davies have all had their tussles with management. There will no doubt be many more. But equally there are many managers who have treated their clients well.

One of the best ways of reducing the possibility of being taken for a ride is to know about the business. Chuck Berry, when asked what he would do differently if he could start his career again, answered: 'I'd take a course in business studies, then become a musician.'

Very few groups opt to be without a manager. They may do at the beginning when they have more time and less need of one, but in the end most find they need someone to organize, hassle, act as go-between, fight the battles and put the group's case to others. It is difficult to be creative one moment then detached enough to act as a manager the next, and if you are successful you simply won't have the time.

Even when you're just starting out you need someone who can take away the pressure of dealing with pub bookers and agents, look after you, nanny you, and most importantly be objective. It is difficult for a band to observe how a set goes, for example, and criticize its order or content. A good manager, as long as he is trusted by the group, can do that.

Jazz Summers, who managed Wham!, says, 'You can't achieve anything in this business unless you have somebody managing you. A record company has to be manipulated. A manager takes ideas from a band and persuades the record company that the band knows what it wants. And you have got to be prepared to be in long-term partnership with your manager. If you can't find an experienced one, find a mate and then come to somebody like me who will dual-manage.'

You need different sorts of manager at different times in your career. If you are lucky, you might find a young manager, probably a friend, who will learn and grow with you. The good managers are usually based in London, but if you are outside the capital you may well start with a local man: then, if you have found the right one, you may find you can get rich together.

It could well be the best thing for a fledgling band to find a local independent manager with, say, six groups who visits London regularly (for example, every three weeks). He might have built up a good rapport with the press and record companies and be able to get some interest in you. The right connections are all-important.

But the time usually comes when you need someone with more clout and know-how than a local man will ever have. Lack of good management is the biggest single factor in holding back talent. John Henry, who runs one of the largest rehearsal rooms in London, comments: 'The biggest sin of all in my mind is seeing a great band with a duff manager rehearsing; I can see their potential, but I know they'll go nowhere. Sometimes I want to step in and point out what is going on, but there's no point. You don't get any thanks until it's too late.'

A good manager is essential if your career is to progress. A bad manager is worse than no manager at all.

Your manager should have the ability to see what the future might hold, and those that can do this are exceptional. Then, when your career starts to roll, you need a manager with experience in making deals. Just going for a huge advance may not be the best step to take at that time, but a good lawyer can help if your manager is inexperienced in this field.

As Ed Bicknell, manager of Dire Straits, puts it: 'You need a manager who can hang on when the roller-coaster starts. That's the worrying time. Most people go into the business because they love it. I did. A good manager will take on a band not for the future kudos and fame and money, but because he likes what he sees and believes in it.

'When I took on Dire Straits, they made it very quickly. I put them into clubs for six months, then they went on the road with Talking Heads. In February 1978 their first album came out and sold 5 million copies. It was the world's biggest-selling début album of all time.

'But the first three years weren't joy and happiness or fun, as many people might think. It was sheer terror and fear because I didn't know if I could hang on to the success or cope with it, or whether the whole pack of cards would collapse. I don't envy a young manager getting success too soon. And you don't get rich quick either. It can take two years for the money to come through.'

There is no course in record business management. It has to be learnt slowly through experience and making mistakes. A would-be manager can't learn it all in a few months; a great deal has to be done by instinct, therefore, before he has acquired that experience.

Obtaining deals is only part of a manager's duties, though swinging first the recording deal, then the publishing one, are obviously of prime importance. There is also an enormous administration job ahead. He should concentrate on co-ordinating his band's career on a worldwide basis, acting as mediator between group and company. Creative bands do not want to see their music sold down the river, so their attitudes and opinions must be taken into account. Managers have to persuade record companies of their group's point of view. Then they have to persuade the rest of the world.

A manager should be someone who enjoys the music business but is not influenced by glamour. Some managers are in it purely for the money; the best ones are those who really care about the music. They have to be able to stand up to record companies, publishers, agents, and so on, and to help educate the group, offer professional advice and act as a responsible friend.

The most important thing when looking for management is to find someone whom you trust. All successful manager/artist relationships have lasted a long time. Cliff Richard has been with Peter Gormley since 1957, Eric Clapton with Roger Forrester from 1965, Elton John and John Reid are still together, and Bruce Springsteen and Jon Landau have been in partnership since Springsteen's early days.

When meeting managers don't be impressed by flash talk or appearances. Arriving to meet you in a large, expensive car and taking you to the best restaurant is not what you are looking for. Don't be overawed by the sort who are all mouth ('I did this, I can do that'): it is what they can do for you that matters. But they and you must be realistic. Be wary of anyone who promises he can get you a marvellous contract within a couple of months. No one can guarantee anything in this business.

When you have found a manager you get on with and who has the right approach for you, you should draw up some sort of agreement. It may not be a full-blown contract. Some managers will take on a group for six months before contracts are signed. Paul King did this when he took on Tears for Fears. That way, when they eventually signed, they both knew it would work.

A manager will usually start by listening to a tape. If he is suitably impressed he will meet the group to see if they are decent people and then see them perform live.

Take time to discuss what you want and find out how the manager sees your career developing. Don't be pushed into signing immediately. The earlier anyone wants you to sign, the more cynical you should be. A manager who is over-eager for you to sign on the dotted line is not necessarily the one for you. Nor can there be any advantage for him in being tied to a band that is not happy with him as a manager.

A manager should be firm, fair and friendly, cool, calm and collected. He should be honest with you and explain how he sees your career progressing. He should be aware of the devious nature of some of the people he will have to deal with and have the ability to counter that.

He must be able to bring together two views which may be far apart – those of a possibly hysterical artist and those of a company for whom making money has to take priority over artistic concerns. He must not be the sort of person who will storm into record companies, publishers' or agents' offices, blow his top and screw up the deal. No company welcomes threatening or unreasonable behaviour, an unpleasant manner or aggressive talk.

In the view of one manager, checking on the record company is a major part of the job: 'You have got to make sure the record company is working for your record. You have to be there all the time, making a nuisance of yourself. I go up once a week to make sure they are continuing to work on our record. Also you can show support for the record company and get feedback.

'It is a very important part of a manager's job to make sure money is not wasted.'

Check out your prospective manager's credentials. Most people in the music business are open to being asked questions. For example, if a manager approaches you, shows interest and says he managed Spandau Ballet, check it out. Think about it: if he's as good as he says he is, how did he find the time to come to a gig of yours and find out about you?

So look up the phone number of the record company in question, speak to the switchboard and ask for the name of (say) Spandau's manager. If the switchboard operator cannot help, ask to speak to someone in the promotion department, who will probably tell you. If the manager said he *used* to manage a particular group, ring up the existing management company and try to speak to whoever is the present manager. Explain who you are, that you have been approached by Joe Smoe, and ask if he can tell you anything about him, in confidence of course.

Despite the dubious image of many people in the music business there are many who *are* honest and don't like to see others get ripped off. So the person you speak to will probably take the time to tell you either, for example, yes, he ripped us off some years ago, or yes, he's a very nice man but couldn't take that band any further, and so on. But don't forget this is only one person's personal opinion; always try to get a second one. At such a time a lawyer can come in handy, as he may well be able to get more truth out of people. People will talk to a professional more freely sometimes because they know the information won't go any further. The lawyer can then let you know whether this second report was generally favourable or not.

When the time comes for contracts it is essential to obtain independent legal advice from a good music-business lawyer. Any respectable manager will encourage you to use a lawyer. Contracts between manager and artist are often rather unspecific, especially in terms of what the manager agrees to do during what period of time, but there are some general guidelines to bear in mind (see pages 147–9).

A manager will charge about 20 per cent of your earnings for his services; higher than 25 per cent is extortionate unless he is also dealing with your publishing and accounting – which he should only do if he has the necessary experience. It is an arguable point whether this 20 per cent is taken from gross (i.e. before costs, including tax, have been subtracted) or net earnings. The manager will obviously want to take it from gross as his percentage will then yield larger earnings. But from your point of view, there will be times when it seems extremely unfair for your manager to make money while you are losing it: for example, touring is usually a loss-making operation, and all the more so if a manager's percentage is taken off before all the expenses have been subtracted.

If you do not have a record deal, your manager should obtain one for you, ideally within the first year; this stipulation could provide the let-out clause in your contract if you are not happy with him. But watch out for a manager who can promise a quick deal and big advance. He may well be adept at obtaining that, but little use thereafter in furthering your career. What you want is that he should take all the worries of the business side of your affairs off your shoulders; in practice, however, it always pays to keep a close eye on what your manager is doing. Just because you have a manager doesn't mean you can throw off all responsibility for your career.

Use your manager – he is there to be your spokesman. When you get uptight – say, about the way your record company is treating you – he should be able to make your demands seem reasonable. A good manager will stop you putting both feet in your mouth.

Never forget that you and your manager are working together for a common aim – your success. Gone are the days when a manager would take a band and mould and manipulate it into his idea of what it should be. Although you are working *with* a manager, he is working *for* you, not the other way round. Don't be bullied by your manager into doing things you do not want to do. Listen to him, but remember it is your career – not his.

The manager/artist partnership is often seen as a marriage rather than as a father/child relationship. If there are problems, there should be a cooling-off period before any decisions are made. There should be a clause in the contract to enable you to break professionally, with notice of x months given on either side, followed by a civilized divorce.

CHAPTER 9

Production and production deals

Producers are the people who can turn your music from a good song into a chart winner. You might think the way you play it is just right, but unless you have the unusual ability of being able to listen to it with complete objectivity, it is unlikely that you will get it absolutely right.

A good producer – such as Trevor Horn, who turned Frankie Goes to Hollywood into a million-selling band – can be worth every penny of his 3-4 per cent rake-off from the record's retail price. A bad producer is a waste of money.

Recording techniques have changed almost out of recognition in the last ten years and you need a competent producer/engineer to use them to your best advantage. These changes have also made recording a far more expensive business – gone is the time when you could record a single for a mere £2000. Now the figure would be nearer £10,000. So it is vital to get that sound right as quickly as possible.

Producers range from the top-flight highly expensive ones to sound engineers who are hoping one day to become fully-fledged producers. Sound engineers can be very helpful when you are starting out, because although they will not have so much expertise they will have listened to many sounds and should be able to provide that objective view you need. And they will, of course, be much cheaper.

When choosing a producer, don't just listen to your record company's suggestions. Go through your record collection, listen to the music you like, note down which producer has worked on which record and go to someone you like and admire. Don't just leave it to others to choose. They may have reasons for going to one specific producer other than those which are in your best interests.

If a record company suggests a particular producer just

because he has produced a couple of singles in the charts, this could spell problems. He will be in demand, and therefore expensive, but not necessarily right for you. Yet some companies tend to think that a 'hot' producer will make any record an instant hit.

If a band wants a producer who is a little out of the ordinary – for example, someone who has not been working in the mainstream recently – it should put his name forward. If the band feels really strongly about it and can give solid reasons why it wants this person, the record company should agree – within reason.

Consider possibilities such as recording outside London, where studios are much cheaper. This will enable you to keep down your production costs. If you find a good studio with a lively engineer, it could work very well. But watch out that you don't pick a bad studio: you could end up with a useless tape. Visit the studio before you book it, listen to a tape that has been recorded there to see what the quality is like, and check that you can get on with the engineer. If he doesn't like your sort of music, he won't do the best job for you.

One London producer talked of the differences in costs between London and the provinces: 'I've just worked with the Rhythm Sisters, who come from Halifax [Yorkshire]. The costs were more in the 'seventies line, because studios are so much cheaper up there. They got to me by one of the band blagging his way down here with a tape. He came in with songs, which were not that great but I could see he had something and he was so determined. His attitude made a lot of difference. Exactly two years from that day I got them a deal with Chrysalis.'

If you are put with a producer you do not know, you must try to work with him, and if you can't, you must say so, otherwise you will never produce your best.

Remember there must be give and take, though not to the extent that you feel compromised. There is no place for arrogance anywhere in the business, and that includes the recording studio. Attitudes like 'It's our record and we know exactly what we want' will get you nowhere. Everyone in recording studios is there to be creative and making a record should be a joint effort. However, the vast majority of bands do change producers at some stage.

When a producer works with a new group each has to find its way around. The band may well have set ideas which it finds difficult to explain lucidly at first. The producer has to find out gradually what the band really wants, by working with them patiently. It is up to the producer and the record company to translate what the band says it wants into what it actually means.

Try not to allow yourselves to be pushed into doing what you feel is wrong. Be strong enough, or use your manager, to say what you feel. The record company should realize that only if you are happy will you be able to work well.

And as one non-record company man put it: 'Be one step ahead of the bastards. Be prepared to be unpopular; a record company will follow the path of least resistance.'

Some producers like to take the control away from the record company – to take on the responsibility of failure or success. Although record company executives (A & R people, usually) often go into the studios with new bands, the final sound really should be for the producer and the band to work out, especially if the record company has hired the producer: presumably it did so because it respected and trusted him.

Production is vital to the success of a record, but it is not the answer to a dull, badly written, incompetently played song. Visuals, too, may count for a lot, but the song is still the thing. Production is therefore very important, although as one music journalist observed, there is a danger that 'eventually production will vanish up its own synthesizer.'

The choice of music you record should be discussed between you and your record company first, then with the producer. Should you go for something new and interesting or a sound similar to what is selling at the moment? There is tremendous apathy from the listening public at present for anything new and challenging. And judging by the number of golden oldies selling – even the Monkees re-forming for a comeback – today's new music is not providing what the public wants.

But this cannot be the case forever. The time is ripe for

something completely different. Historically this happens every ten years, but there has been no sign of any major new sound or movement in this decade.

PRODUCTION COMPANIES

Many producers have now progressed from just being employed on an *ad hoc* basis by a group or record company. They act like an A & R department, in that they find groups before they get a record deal, record a demo with them and sell that to the record companies. This can be a good way to proceed, as – back to the contacts again – a known producer will have more influence with a record company than an unknown group.

Small production companies are more likely to take a gamble – to see a band and produce something quickly – whereas big companies can take months to make up their minds.

It may be said that production companies are doing the job a major record company would have done ten years ago. They are taking very new groups, working on them and with them, building them up and then selling them to the general public. For the group, one advantage in doing a production deal rather than going with a small independent record company which will treat you in a similar way is that the production company will have the incentive to get you that major recording deal which should elicit more money and more power. It is just another way of getting there.

Major record companies like things this way as it leaves the production company to take the risk, spend the money and do the first bit of hard work. They then can take on the finished product, if they so wish. Ten to fifteen years ago a major record company would have done this itself, employing the very people who have now set up on their own.

Charles Gillett, who has been in the music business for a long time in a variety of roles, including producer, manager, agent, publisher and DJ, sees it this way: 'If a group is any good and it is ready, it will attract the attention of a major label. Production people like myself take groups a couple of years earlier. We act as a sounding board. I will pay for a demo, with the aim of recovering the money from a record company or third party. If not, I will recoup the income from the writer. We usually form a publishing relationship with the group, with options to publish for quite a long time.

'If we are talking about a few hundred pounds, we will do it as publishers. If it's over £1000, we'll form a separate recording arrangement. And we do take a larger cut than bigger publishers, because we work with fewer people, but we have a more personal approach.

'I usually put a time limit on the deal, for instance that we will aim to have a recording deal within a year; if no deal, then that agreement finishes. Bands should send us tapes. Most people like to see bands live, but I work differently. I have taken quite a few punts on tapes, where the group was not ready to perform live but I've liked what I've heard and have thought it had something. I've had a couple of successes like that, but also a few which haven't worked. That's the risk.'

PRODUCTION DEALS

There are many different types of production deal, some of which are described below. One producer says that though he used to go to gigs, he rarely does so now: 'I hear groups on cassettes, but only if they have been recommended. If I like the sound, I'll meet the people, put them into the studio for a day and see how they sound live. There'll be no charge for that. If they are any good I will make three or four tracks for a demo, often reworking the tracks if need be.

'With demo and pictures I'll make an assault on the majors. What normally happens is that they say, OK, but can you do more tracks? and they'll want to see the band live. So you're probably looking at three to four months later before a single is discussed.'

Another producer with his own studio says: 'I might see a band at a gig, or their manager. I will go and see them and initially do a quick demo to see how good they are in the studio and whether they are worth pursuing.

'We work on three production options. One: if the demo

tape is good enough on its own I would take that tape to a record company. Two: the band could be nearly good enough to be funded by a record company but not quite, so I might get funding from a publishing company, then go back to the record company, knowing the band has a publishing deal which makes it more interesting, or use the money to record again. Three: we would fund the band fully; record a song as the master and sell it as the finished product. This way we could sign on a lower-level deal, for just a one-off single; we would not need the money up front because we would not be signing for a single and album.

'If I felt strongly about the band, I would record immediately. Going with a major means it can take at least six months to get into the studio.'

The idea of selling the finished product used to be very popular in the 'seventies; then the record companies went off the idea, but they have recently started coming back to it. Now it is not unknown for bands to make whole albums because it is so easy to have a home studio. This is especially the case in the USA and becoming more common in Britain.

'We treat deals with bands very much as record companies would,' explains the same producer. 'We give our time for free, so we expect bands to sort themselves out, find accommodation, etc. When we get a deal with a record company, we sort out a deal and take a percentage of the advance, instead of charging the band for studio time *pro rata*.' This is a good arrangement for a band, because it makes the cost of studio time the producer's gamble rather than the band's.

Another producer suggests that there are four different ways for a group to do a production deal. If it has already signed with a major label, the label may approach the production company. Otherwise, the production company itself may see the group and push it towards a certain label, with a recommendation and an indication that it will produce the first single. Alternatively, the group may find a production company who will work with it and build it up. Or the production company will immediately produce the group and obtain a recording deal for it.

'Fees are always negotiable,' stresses another producer. 'Normally with a new band if there is interest from the majors we will do a record on a simple basis. Or we will spend time and money putting the band in a studio. That is our gamble. If we then find no interest, that is our loss. If we get a deal, we ask for the normal producer's royalty of 3 per cent and our costs back. The advantage for groups of doing things this way is that because a record company has been offered a finished product, the single or album advances and royalty splits are likely to be better. The group is in a stronger position.'

If the split of royalties from the record company is 10 per cent to the performer and 3 per cent to the producer, for example, the advance will be divided similarly.

Some production companies will sign a deal with the group and then lease the master tape to major recording companies. The production company signs a contract with the record company and pays the group a royalty after production costs have been taken off. If this is the case the artists should have to sign a letter saying they have read and understood the producer's contract with the record company.

Solicitors are wary of production deals, however, and there can be a problem if the producer is spending a lot of money on your behalf which you have to repay. This might sound OK to begin with, but if you are given an advance of, say, £50,000 and find that you owe £20,000 to the producer, £5000 for old studio time and £10,000 for equipment, you will be left with £15,000 for all of you to live on for the year.

This is not unreasonable but it is something to bear in mind. One eminent lawyer advises: 'Watch production deals. You can get into a situation where a manager has his own production company, to which he signs you, thereby putting himself into a difficult position – wanting to do the best for both companies. It can lead to enormous trouble and shouldn't be done.'

The following is a good example of a bad production deal. A band walked into a local 16-track studio to do some demos on a production agreement. The demos were free at the time, but when the band got its recording deal the money was taken out of the advance. The producer in fact took his money before the group got its hands on it. So the band ended up with nothing.

So be wary of taking money or free time for demos (or other purposes) if it is offered, as you will only have to pay it back later; and of letting the producer take your publishing (as well as his production percentage on the recording deal) without giving you an advance.

It can take a long time, possibly years, to sort out debts like those, and means you will be forever fighting over the past. It could even ruin you and your creativity forever. Seeing everything you have fought for going down the pan may make you depressed and stop you working. The message seems to be, once again, by all means look into the deal, but proceed with caution and always seek professional advice.

CHAPTER 10

Agents, promoters, bookers

A good agent looks after a band's live career, builds up grass-roots support and arranges tours; he frequently acts as a mediator, attempting to keep three parties happy – the band, the manager and the record company. The importance of the agent has greatly increased in recent years, and it is often essential to have one even to secure a one-off gig or play a pub or club date.

A promoter, on the other hand, books and pays bands for a particular venue, organizes and publicizes the event, usually working with agents – and slowly the jobs of agent and promoter are merging. (In America a promoter is not allowed to act as an agent, but that is not the case in the UK.)

A booker is usually someone who is employed by one venue that engages live acts. He or she is the person you need to persuade if you want to play in that particular place.

An agent will take from 10 to 15 per cent of your live earnings. So why can't you do it yourself? You probably can when starting out and playing the very small venues – pubs and small local clubs. But when you reach the larger circuits you will find that bookers often deal only through agents. Although frustrating for you, it can be advantageous, for if an agent takes you on his books he may be able to persuade a good venue to book you, on the understanding that it can also have one of the agent's bigger acts.

If you are new and have not had time to build up a following, you can either employ a small agent working in your area to help you or you can do it yourself. In the latter case, someone in the band must be prepared to act as agent. And that means time – a lot of wasted time, working through lists of gigs, telephoning, telephoning back and telephoning again: systematically contacting every venue you think is right for you. If you miss one out, you might as well not bother at all. It could be that one which takes you and provides the start or opportunity you need. You can never afford to miss that chance.

But if you haven't got a record deal you will find it difficult to get an agent, and if you can't play the bigger venues, attainable only through an agent, you might well not get the attention of a record company: so you could find yourself in a catch-22 situation.

One reason why agents prefer to deal with bands already signed to a record label is because it is easier for them to deal with fellow professionals. As one agent explained: 'Groups rarely know what is best for them – where and how much to play. Ideally we like to have bands with a major record company and a strong manager.'

As a band, you should find out which acts an agent handles. Would you fit in? Do you like what the other bands do? Go with the agent you want to go with and feel you can get on with rather than the one your record company might push you towards. And don't sign a contract with the agency immediately. Get it to put in three or four dates for you, then discuss the situation. If the agency is really keen it will probably want to sign you up for three to five years. So unless you are really happy with it and have seen what it can do, don't sign.

Now that even some of the pubs and small clubs have been sewn up by agents, promoters often get involved as well. This could mean that even if you have booked the gig originally yourself you may find that you are expected to pay 20 per cent to the promoter. There is little you can do about it if you want to play that particular venue.

Agents operate by assessing a band, working out what level of gig (pubs, small clubs or college circuit, for example) it should play at, and then striving to book it into the right places.

One agent explained: 'A band has two careers – live and recording. If the band is a good live band it can earn enough money to survive. Often record companies don't understand the importance of playing live. Or that sometimes it is wrong for a particular band. Or that some venues only suit particular bands.'

Some agencies go for bands which are likely to have hit singles, so they get a fast turnover. Others try to build bands on a long-term basis, and in a band's early career will work closely with its record company.

Agents will also go out and look for bands, either approaching direct those that interest them or dealing with managers they know and trust. For example, if an agent is handling a hit band signed to a particular manager, he might be persuaded to take on a new band the manager has found.

In the late 1960s promoters got a bad name for ripping people off, though that happens less frequently nowadays. In those days many of the mainstream promoters had started as owners of large clubs who would pay very little money. Now the power is much more equitably distributed, although you won't find many poor promoters. It is quite a static area of activity: in 1986 only two new promoters of any note came into the business in Britain. But there is no training for a promoter, nor are there any regulations governing a promoter's behaviour. Anyone can become one, and as a band you have no way of checking how honest a particular promoter might be other than by asking around. A promoters' association has recently been formed, but as yet it has very few teeth.

Promoters take the financial risk on a booking – not the band. It is very unusual for a band to lose out. If the whole promotion company should suffer a catastrophe the band might be out of pocket, but that has only happened once in the last ten years. Paul Loasby, for example, lost thousands of pounds on the disastrous Barry Manilow open-air gig at Blenheim Palace in 1984.

The major promoters do not deal with very small gigs, because it would not pay them. For example, one admitted: 'The smallest gig we would deal with would be something like the Purcell Room [on the South Bank], which holds 300 people, but only if it were connected with larger gigs. We usually wouldn't deal with a capacity below 800 to a thousand people. We need to be guaranteed £500 for ourselves before taking on a promotion.'

A promoter takes a huge risk every time he stages an event, whereas an agent does not. The agent organizes and arranges tour dates, but is not putting any money up front and is earning commission from a percentage of the band's earnings, or an agreed fee. The promoter, on the other hand, takes a gamble. He has to work out in advance what seat prices to charge (which is not difficult for an experienced promoter), how much to pay the band and how much, if any, percentage to give the band from the seat price. He then has to put money up to book the hall, organize security and safety measures, and pander to the band's every whim – from a certain size of dressing room and number of security men on duty to crates of special beer and unusual foods. (One artist is rumoured to demand packets of Smarties, with all the brown ones removed, in his dressing room before every performance.)

If the seats do not sell, if the promoter has forgotten something vital or if he has estimated the prices wrongly, he will lose out. It is not difficult to make mistakes if you do not know what you are doing. Booking a hall which is too small or too big, overlooking certain safety regulations or discovering that there is no existing music licence for that specific venue could jeopardize the gig.

As Paul Crockford, who promotes Dire Straits, amongst others, says: 'You have to know what you are doing – which area and venue, for example, will be right for a group. We don't often book new groups, but we will do favours for the large bands. For example, Dire Straits specifically wanted one little support band, so we arranged it for them.'

Promoters usually find their groups from agents. Agents ring up and say: 'We are booking a tour. Do you fancy taking so-and-so group for a few days? We want to tour in such-and-such an area.' Then the promoter goes round finding free venues, costs the tour and sends the agents a costing, also suggesting an appropriate fee for the band.

The agent may persuade a promoter to take a new band on his books as support. This is another reason why getting on to an agent's books with a few good names is worth while. He has the power to pull the strings: as unknown performers, you do not.

Quite often, you will get more than one promoter on a tour, each one knowing a specific area. If they are fighting against each other for a band, the promoters will often get together and agree to split the profit. It also makes it cheaper for them to set up.

The sorts of duties a promoter undertakes are, for example, providing casual labour, organizing the catering, arranging press coverage, advertising and posters, and so on. All costs will come off the takings before any profits are apportioned.

You can, of course, promote yourselves as performers, but, understandably, established promoters are not keen to encourage this. 'It is not good for the industry, big bands promoting themselves,' explained one. 'There is no incentive to a promoter, if he is thinking about taking on a newish band but suspects he will not be getting the money when it is successful.' Bands usually stay with a particular promoter if they are happy with him.

The only safe situation for doing it yourselves would be if you were guaranteed a seat sell-out. After all, it is difficult for a promoter to shout at himself, and mistakes are easily made. Spandau Ballet, for example, promote themselves and always have done. But in the early days when one Spandau member forgot to order a barrier a gig failed to go ahead. Nobody had told him and he had not thought about that particular point.

It is normal for a promoter to guarantee a fee to a band plus a percentage over and above expenses if the gig is successful. Agents take a cut of that, usually about 20 per cent and the manager also takes his 15-20 per cent, depending on whether he is taking a percentage from the gross or the net income. Bands pay all their own expenses, from supplying the PA to hotel bills, travel, and so on. So the gig must be very successful if the band is to make any money.

If a manager is very inefficient the promoter will also organize all the travel, hire, etc. but it is not very cost-effective for him.

CHAPTER 11

Pluggers

A plugger's job is to alert the relevant radio and television programmes to your new record. Without his persistence and his contacts, the record may die a quiet death regardless of its worth. Many record executives are very scathing about pluggers – their abilities, their fees, their performance – but without them new singles wouldn't see the light of day.

As one record executive puts it: 'A good plugger is worth his weight in gold. But I consider them to be an evil necessity, because new records need to be brought to the attention of producers and I have never been involved with a record taking off without its having been plugged. You need people who have built up relationships with the producers.'

The quantity of product being produced – over 100 new records are released every week in Britain – is overwhelming, and although your record may be outstanding a gentle or hefty push from someone whom the producers know and respect will give it an edge. A producer can't possibly listen to them all so the plugger acts as a sifting machine.

There are both independent pluggers, who work for any label who will employ them, and most importantly whose records they like; and in-house pluggers, who work solely for one record company. The major record companies usually have their own full-time plugger. As an A & R director of one of the largest majors says: 'In-house pluggers are vitally important. They are a crucial part of the company. Freelance pluggers don't give a damn. They take a record on and if it gets played they take the credit.'

In the music-business hierarchy pluggers range from the lowest of the low to highly respected operators, taking their job further than just the haranguing of producers. They get involved with the early development of a band, give advice on the best way of promoting the record and oversee all the promotion. They choose what TV and radio the band should do and work closely with it.

One plugger who works like this explains: 'We are always employed by a record company. If we were hired by the artist's management there could be problems. We need to have direct access to the artist.'

Some pluggers have diversified into finding and promoting brand-new bands. Because of their contacts, they should have more luck in taking tapes round to record companies, getting live recording sessions and other forms of exposure than an unheard-of band would.

If your record company employs a plugger, it pays for him. Promotion and marketing are two costs that are not clawed back from the artist. If you are employing a plugger yourself, however, you should expect to pay a set charge plus incentives. This is not a bad idea, as it should ensure he works hard on your record for you. The biggest problem is never actually knowing what the plugger does.

Some charge by radio play: for example, £50 each time your record is broadcast. Most receive chart bonuses, too, operating for, say, the top 75, the top 50 and top twenty, etc. If the record makes no. 1, the plugger can earn a lot. Top pluggers can earn £1000 a record; a no. 1 can put it up to £5000. Some take royalties, which can work well if the plugger really believes in a record as he will usually take it on for a low fee, relying on royalties to boost his earnings.

It is most important for a plugger to believe in the record he is plugging, and not just be doing it for a fee. But this can be very hard to establish. So it is worth talking to more than one, and working out a reasonable deal. Don't just accept what they demand: if a plugger likes your record you will be able to come to some agreement.

Don't waste money on pluggers who will not devote enough time to your record. The plugger is working for you, remember. When looking for a plugger, check his track record first: don't give him any money before you have done so. If he or she says, 'I can get you ten plays next week on Radio 1', take no notice. No one can ever guarantee that.

A good plugger will have been in the business several years, be able to prove that he has been instrumental in the success of several records and have contacts in all the right places. Pluggers have to be devoted to their work, and for most of the good ones it is their life. Even outside their working hours they will be socializing with producers and record company executives who have become mates over the years, and it is this familiarity which gives them the 'in' when it is needed.

Pluggers still have to make appointments to see producers, but a little wining and dining never come amiss. All producers will deny that they can be influenced by bribes, whether it be a free lunch, drugs or a holiday in the sun. But it would be an extraordinary world if this were absolutely true.

In the end everything rests on the quality of the product the plugger is trying to promote. Very few pluggers of any note will take on a record indiscriminately. They will listen to it first, quite often go to see you play live as well, and if they like the record and you agree their terms they will take it on, usually for a period of six to eight weeks.

They will try one producer three or four times if they do not elicit a definite yes at first. If the reaction is no, there is not much they can do, and if three or four attempts produce nothing, carrying on will be a waste of their time and your money.

What do pluggers look for in a record? First, they have to be able to get it played, so it has to be commercial, or to have a special angle such as having been produced by somebody well-known, or featuring a performer who has been in a well-known band: any such 'handle' helps them to sell it to a producer.

Of course, the plugger's opinion of your record is a personal one, so do not get dispirited if you get a bad reaction from the first one you approach. Until you have tried every 'decent' plugger around, you must not give up.

One prominent Radio 1 producer says: 'Sometimes I get bands ringing up, but not often. Records are pushed mostly through pluggers. The pluses of pluggers are that they appreciate the demands on one's time, especially when you're doing a strip show like *Simon Bates*. They come in, give a short preamble, play the record, and there's a little more chat after. It probably takes no more than 15 minutes.

'A good plugger can act as a filter. He or she gives a quick breakdown of the band and the single, fixes interviews with a band and basically takes all the hassle away. He acts as an intermediary between Radio 1 and the band.

'But the amount of rubbish some pluggers push is extraordinary. I don't understand how some of them get employed.'

Getting a hard-working plugger will help if the record is good but if it isn't the best plugger in the world won't make any difference.

One top plugger explains how he sees his job: 'Contacts are most important. The same people will use you over and over again to plug records. A record company will send tapes to six promotion people, get their reactions and go from there, while artists' managements tend to want their own plugger. I get a record one week before release and I am paid generally on a fee and chart bonus. I see producers once or twice a week. If a producer likes the record but it does not get on the A playlist, it will go on B list. Because record companies know they have four weeks of play if the record is on the playlist, they will saturate the shops with the record.' And once that has happened, everything depends on the final arbiter – the public.

When pluggers are pushing a record and it starts creeping up the charts, they pay great attention to its placing. The mid-week BBC/Gallup chart is put out on Fridays at 12.30 p.m. The main weekly chart is published on Tuesdays. The mid-week one is pretty accurate, within five places, and a plugger will know from that exactly what to do with any particular record.

You could try plugging your own record, if you can't afford the services of a professional plugger, but it will take all your time and energies just to make the appointments. You will need to find out the correct names of all the producers for Radio 1, BBC and the commercial television stations, Capital, Radio London and the bigger out-of-town local radio stations. Then be prepared to hang around at their offices for hours before being seen. You will only get a few minutes, so forget all the flannel. Introduce yourself and be prepared for the producer to listen to only a few seconds of the record. He will be experienced enough to know, that fast, whether it is right for him. He may not listen to it at the time, but put it on a large pile to listen to later.

Even so, you will find it hard trying to check out afterwards what his reaction was. No producer would ever go to the trouble of letting all the individuals who send in unsolicited tapes know what he thinks of their record.

The best guarantee of getting plays is still to have a good record, well packaged so that it attracts programme producers' attention. Do not bother to send very detailed biographies with the record: they are a waste of your and the producer's time.

It is very rarely worth just turning up at a producer's office on the off-chance. This might have worked ten years ago, but most producers and presenters are now far too busy to see people without appointments – and there are too many people trying to see them this way. Some DJs will take the time to speak to people who approach them unannounced, but not many. Anne Nightingale, for example, whose show is not playlisted (see below), has a liberal view of people trying to push their own records.

'People do hang around outside Radio 1 trying to approach DJs. I consider it part of our job to listen and talk, and it's nice to meet them. I feel they have taken the trouble to come here and wait for me, so the least I can do is to spend a small amount of time with them. I get stopped everywhere and given records, and asked if I will play them. But a record has to knock me out, it has to be brilliant, for me to play it. If it is, I will.'

The reason air play is so vital is because records need to be heard over and over again. How often do you hate a record on first hearing but after hearing it three or four times find it has grown on you? So the more your record is aired the better.

Daytime shows sell records; night-time ones do not. The most important shows for plays at present (all BBC) are therefore *The Breakfast Show, Mike Smith, Steve Wright, Peter Powell* and *Simon Bates*. On the television it is important to have your record played on *Whistle Test, The Chart Show*, breakfast television and the Saturday children's shows. Other radio programmes which help, but are not renowned for generating huge sales, are *Gary Crowley, Janice Long* and *John Peel*.

How does the mysterious Radio 1 playlist work? There are 50 records on the A list, and each week ten are taken off and ten are put on. Chosen records are guaranteed to be played for four weeks from 10 to 25 times a week. Records on the longer B list can be played from 0 to 8 times: it is really an aide-memoire. The all-important playlist operates from 5.30 a.m. to 7.30 p.m. each day.

The playlist meeting, which takes place once a week on Thursdays at 10 a.m. and finishes at about 1 p.m., is attended by the producers of the major strip shows (*Simon Bates, Mike Smith, Peter Powell*, etc.) and the specialist producers of, for example, rock, reggae and soul programmes. Mike Hawkes, Janice Long's producer, is also there.

By the start of each meeting each producer will have endeavoured to have listened to all the records released that week. In one week, for example, there might be 107 singles released. Each participant at the meeting in turn puts forward a record he thinks strong enough to go on the A list: that might be 50 records in all. Then they listen to all of them again and make the final decision. The ten records which are added to the list are chosen basically on the strength of how good they sound on radio Those which do not warrant heavy play go on to the B list.

CHAPTER 12

The charts

When you've finally managed to get a single or an album released, its eventual placing (should you be so lucky) in the charts will be all-important, both for this release and for your future success.

There are several charts on which your record might appear, depending on its style and type. So how do the charts work? And how fair are they? The UK music charts first appeared in 1952. They were very basic, covering 78s in the main, and were simply based on information supplied by a few record dealers who were telephoned for the purpose.

In 1969 the first independent chart was set up. This was financed by the BBC, the music trade paper of the day (now *Music Week*) and several record companies. It was produced by the British Market Research Bureau. In those days information was sent by post from 250 record shops, until the demise of the Sunday postal service. Then a faster courier service was used. The information was produced from a diary system and was obviously open to widespread abuse.

Gallup took over from BMRB in 1983 and in 1987 renewed the licence for another three to four years. The BPI (British Phonographic Industry) pays 50 per cent of the cost, *Music Week*, which publishes the chart, pays 38 per cent, and the BBC (for *Top of the Pops*) pays 12 per cent. The chart compilation is completely computerized and virtually, but not absolutely, hype-proof. That makes it an expensive operation: it will cost £2.2 million for the next three years, which is nearly £¾ million per year.

Any BPI member can subscribe to the Gallup chart. This weighty document, issued weekly, lists the top 200 singles and top 200 albums – LPs and cassettes – including details of chart positions for the previous week and the three before that, number of weeks in the chart, label, record company, distributor, catalogue number and percentage increase or decrease in sales. Gallup at present charges £300 per year for this service.

Each week a quarter of a million sales are recorded from a panel of 250 shops distributed throughout Britain, from the huge chains such as Woolworth to smaller independent outlets. In fact the BPI has now agreed to double the panel size over the next few years. Sales information is received through the week to be processed by Friday, thereby providing a mid-week sales trend. On Friday a check panel of 125 shops (taken from a list of 600 independent stores and altered each week) is informed of the titles potentially climbing the charts within the top 120 singles. On Monday morning each is telephoned by a Gallup interviewer for his sales report on the previous week's performance of the specified records. These figures are then entered into the computer, balanced and compared with the information from the chart panel.

Any sales of a record which show up as being far higher at the chart panel than the check panel are discounted. Likewise, any sales that are not representative of the total sales pattern are discounted. If there are any serious indications that sales are being tampered with Gallup will alert the BPI, which will investigate that claim. Tampering could mean anything from a group's grannies buying up records in bulk to free gifts (T-shirts, posters, even videos) being given away with the record. Records sold with free gifts are ineligible for the chart, with the following exceptions: promotional items for the group or artist concerned (badges, buttons, sew-on patches, etc.) or a disc or tape by the same group or artist. The distinction is carefully maintained. For example, a couple of thousand copies of the single 'Hey, Fred, You Need a Sun Bed' by Skanga were sold with a small sachet of sun-tan cream attached and were therefore discounted because the sachets, although worth only a few pence, were deemed to be an incentive to the dealer to stock the record and did not promote the artist.

Gallup, if it so wishes, may remove a record from the chart, though this is rarely done. If the case for tampering is proved the BPI can fine the company concerned. If a record is removed from the charts, the record company will be informed and provided with the reasons.

The finished weekly chart is produced during Monday evening and released at 7.45 a.m. on Tuesday. This generates the busiest time of the week for record company, publisher and plugger alike, as well as for radio and TV programme planners.

Let's look at one week's chart panel sales for a real record, chosen at random, to show how many records you might need to sell (in the panel shops, not overall) to get into the charts. No. 1 has 5259 panel sales, no. 2 3682 sales, and no. 3 3530 sales. The difference between nos. 4 and 10 is 1400 sales. From 15 to 50 the difference between some placings is as little as two records, averaging from 10 to 15 sales. And no. 50 has sold only 250 records. The bottom of the pile, no. 200, has made a chart entry with the grand sum of 15 sales.

A member of Gallup comments: 'I consider hype in the form of cheating, such as groups/record companies buying copies of their own records, to be only a very minor irritant. But we are still concerned with the relatively small panel of chart shops. These are quite visible. They have Datapoint systems, and are better supplied by the record companies, which increases sales and therefore distorts the final results. Having the alternative panel, the check panel, does keep that problem within reasonable bounds. But the long-term solution is to increase the panel, and so we are delighted that the BPI has agreed to double its size.

'This also gives us the ability to analyse data more accurately and in more varied ways.'

The Gallup chart is still the one that carries most weight, is watched by the industry and bands alike and is the chart by which success, on the whole, is measured.

There is also the Network chart, compiled for Capital Radio and broadcast simultaneously by all independent radio stations on Sunday afternoons. Publications often reproduce this chart, usually 'because the Gallup chart is copyright and expensive,' as one spokesman commented. 'There are indications that the Network chart has gained credibility and is not so easy to hype. It is more accurate and more up to date and responds to new bands a little better.'

New Musical Express, *Melody Maker* and *Record Mirror* carry their own specialized charts – disco, reggae, soul, US, European, etc. There is also the Independent chart. For a record to be eligible for this chart it has to be released and distributed on an independent label. An independently released record being distributed by one of the major companies may not be included.

The Network chart is compiled by the MRIB (Media Research and Information Bureau) from a cross-section of 300 shops, made up from national multiples, regional chains and independents. It is concerned with singles only, and a small weighting is applied according to the amount of air play the record has received. MRIB is notified as to what has been played on radio each week, so movement in the charts is slightly accentuated if a record is being played a great deal.

As a Capital spokesman says: 'All this does is slightly accelerate movement up and down – and that makes the charts more exciting.

'The Network chart is also compiled on different days from the Gallup/BBC chart. It is put together on Thursday and the top thirty is broadcast on Sunday. The Gallup chart has its cut-off mid-week, so by the time it is published it is a few days out of date. And it is not broadcast on the radio until the Sunday following the Tuesday. Ours is more up to date, and although we are not a national station the top thirty broadcast does go out across all commercial stations at the same time on Sunday, as well as on a few stations abroad.'

For the Network chart a complete checklist of all current chart-eligible titles is sent to the panel members each week. The weekly sales period runs from Thursday to Wednesday. Each outlet is phoned on Thursday to gather the sales information, which is fed into a computer. There is a compensation system for regional and type-of-shop sales irregularities (that is, extra-high sales in the band's local area or in specialist outlets) and the check panel is contacted if anything particularly unusual crops up. The listing covers the top one hundred singles.

The specialized charts are also compiled by the MRIB and researched weekly as follows: each week a computerized checklist of all current titles relevant to the particular chart is mailed to a panel of 75 nationwide retail outlets; MRIB phones each dealer for his sales information on a specified day and the results are collated on computer.

CHAPTER 13

The media

The media may not have a great impact on increasing record sales, but they certainly play a part in the building of a new band and in keeping its profile high when it becomes successful. In the 'sixties, pre-Radio 1, pre-disco and pre-video, the specialist music papers and magazines had more power than they do now. Bands relied much more heavily on touring to build up a following, and the music press could be relied upon to cover the tours. A group's progress to fame and fortune would tend to be slower than it is today.

Music papers and magazines now have less room to devote to covering new groups, especially those without recording contracts. The record companies are largely responsible. As companies spend more and more money on selected high-priority groups, they need to speed up the return on their ever-increasing investments, and one way is by publicity – creating a buzz about the groups. Therefore the record companies put pressure on the media to devote space to those few bands, either by persuading them that the artists are outstanding or have a story worth pursuing, or through gentle bribery, such as wining and dining the relevant journalist, or, immorally, by threatening to withdraw their valuable advertising.

Today most national newspapers carry a rock column, although because of their wider audience they tend to go for stories about the established stars. With the advent of the rock video, sparked off in 1976 by Queen's spectacular 'Bohemian Rhapsody' video, more TV programmes than ever feature rock music.

A mention in a music paper or magazine is vital at the beginning of a band's career, to spread its name and get a buzz going. If it has a record coming out, press coverage will be particularly valuable for export sales. If the band can get a review in the *New Musical Express*, for example, that will make it easier for it to get gigs.

One music paper's editor says: 'The music press is important now, especially for the newer acts. Outside *John Peel* and *Janice Long*, and certain independent and local stations, minority music doesn't get a look in. The media aren't geared to minority acts. The Mighty Lemon Drops, for example, will never get Radio 1 daytime play unless they get a good hit single, but they will get the front page of *Sounds*, so they can get exposure that way.

'It is an ironic situation. We have an uneasy relationship with the majors. All music papers and rock tabloids peaked in about 1980. Now we are all struggling to get a market share of the advertising, so the majors think they can apply pressure. But the music press can often uncover new talent before them. We get lots of calls from A & R departments asking whether a band we have written about has a manager, is signed up, where it's based, etc. And if there is a consensus of opinion between *NME, Sounds* and *Melody Maker*, the record companies are especially interested. One group was raved about by all three, and because of that they were picked up by *The Tube*.'

When encouraging the press to write about you, do be careful about building up a picture which is far beyond what you can actually present. Unless a band can live up to expectations, high-powered promotion can work against it.

One member of Blue Rondo recalls: 'When I joined the band, there was a huge amount of hype happening. They had managed to get an enormous buzz about themselves and what they could and would do. We had to rehearse madly to reach the standard they had put themselves forward to be. We had to do gigs at pubs under a different name until we were good enough. The band was so hyped, the first record zoomed up the charts and I thought we were going to get on *Top of the Pops*, but we just missed doing so.'

And look at Sigue Sigue Sputnik, one of the most hyped groups of 1986. They were on the front page of the *Sun* even before they had a record out. They looked marvellous, behaved appallingly, shocked people quite successfully at a time when it was hard to think that anyone could really be shocked again – but the songs just weren't there. The group simply failed to live up to expectations. If it had been given more time, rather than being pushed into the spotlight practically overnight, it might possibly have lingered a little longer.

It is important to work out how many magazines, newspapers, radio and television shows you can afford to contact, how many tapes or cassettes you can afford to give away and which outlets are worth approaching – which ones will take your music seriously, in other words. Concentrate on them, rather than going for blanket coverage. It costs money to provide copies of tapes, biographies and good pictures and it is vital that you make as professional an impression as you can. Sending in scraps of paper carrying hand-written information about the band, a muzzy tape and blurred picture will not do. If anything is likely to be binned straight away, that will.

Never forget you are competing against hundreds of other eager and able new bands. Presentation is not something to be taken lightly and first impressions, in particular, count for a lot, even though it is your music that has to stand the final test.

How do the people who work on the different magazines, newspapers and programmes see the business? The following pages will provide some insight into how they are likely to regard you as a novice band or solo artist.

SPECIALIST MUSIC PRESS

There are both newspapers and glossy magazines covering popular music. The latter concentrate on the bigger bands, the exclusives and the colour pictures. As a new band, you are unlikely to get a mention without having a single out, but if you have a good story or outstanding picture you might wangle a mention before the record becomes a hit, if it ever does.

Tom Hibbert, deputy editor of *Smash Hits*, a glossy magazine, explains: 'A year ago a band had to be in the charts to get a mention in the magazine. Now we have gone out on a limb and do cover acts which have not had a hit. We wrote about the Housemartins before they made it. Groups must have a record out, though. It is no good contacting us before that stage.

'We have an effect in shaping people's opinions, but would never affect actually what they buy; even if we do a bad review, that doesn't stop the fans buying it. But we do bring names to people's attention.'

Alan Lewis, editor of *No. 1*, says: 'If you want coverage in magazines remember to provide really good photos with a succinct, short, funny press release. If you continue to bombard a magazine, it will have an effect and with luck your name will stick out over the rest of the dross.' (Sending in good pictures is certainly essential for the glossy pop magazines, but as to 'bombarding' them – you would run the risk of boring them stupid.)

Alan Lewis adds: 'Putting in personal appearances is important. People might not like it a lot if you go to their offices, but if you are pleasant they will remember you and probably write an article, if there is a good story. Remember, press want to speak to the band, not its manager. It is easy to think, if you have a manager, that he can do everything, but firstly he won't, and secondly he can't. People seem to be embarrassed now to do things on their own.'

If an article appears, do ring up to say thanks. That's just basic human courtesy, but it is so often forgotten. It will also make the magazine look favourably on the group.

Check the publications you are thinking of approaching to see whether they have a general review editor, who covers all types of newly released music, or specialist writers.

Tony Stewart, the editor of *Sounds*, says: 'We will write about any new band, whether they have a record deal or are just gigging around. Our editorial stance is that we have to do pieces on known bands to keep our commercial viability, but a good proportion of the paper is given over to new bands. If there's a good story angle we'll write about them, as we would if one of the writers particularly liked a group.

'If you are trying to create some interest about a new band and have got a tape, send that in. To get a review of a gig, ring up the editor of the performance section. It doesn't matter if you're out of London: we have correspondents all over the country. Give a selection of dates.

'We also have a news section which covers tour news – we'll put in any dates – and "Nightshift", which is a national gig guide. Anything you want to put in, we will.'

The *New Musical Express*, the long-established 'newspaper' of rock, is far more sectionalized and it is vital to get your music to the right person, otherwise it will get lost. Stuart Cosgrove is its media editor: 'We are sent hundreds of tapes and new singles. Bands should identify with a specific writer within the paper and send it to the right person – however individual a group may think it is, it will fit into some specific general form of music – post-punk, rock, hip-hop, funk, etc. – so get it right.

'Occasionally we do a round-up of local bands, covering the unsigned ones in one specific area. Otherwise we tend to review and interview groups who have record deals of some kind. But we don't make a distinction between major and indi labels, so if a one-man label from Grimsby puts out one local record and there's lots of buzz, we might interview that group. For example, Goodbye Mr MacKenzie brought out one 12-inch and had no track record. One writer on the *NME* liked them and wrote a page and a half on them. And this alerts A & Rs to the single. I would suggest bands send us pix and bios if they have them.'

The *NME* puts out cassettes occasionally, covering the best of young unsigned bands or those on a small label. The 1986 cassette, C86, featured about 16 bands. The bands are given studio facility expenses and a nominal fee. The biggest advantage of these cassettes is the publicity. It can act as a showcase for you and helps to validate your worth.

Music Week, which is the music business's trade paper, covers new groups which have a record out and features a few new ones in its performance section. Nigel Hunter of *Music Week* says: 'If a band or singer is really good it could be worth sending a tape to the A & R section, asking them to come down to a gig, especially if the band is supporting. It might get a review, and everything helps with creating a buzz in the business.'

Jim Reid of *Record Mirror* says his problem is getting to the bands. 'Getting something out of new bands now is really difficult. Even getting *to* them is impossible; there are so many people involved with a band now to get around – lawyers, managers, record companies, all of whom you have to check with first. Big Audio Dynamite were a joy to deal with. I think it had something to do with having a manager from the punk era who believes there is something powerful about music, and that his band should be easy to get to. They are prepared to take risks. Many are not.'

No. 1 was set up purely as a chart paper, but even it is now more aware of new bands. Alan Lewis, its editor, says, 'Like everyone we are searching for the next big thing. Frankly I would say to a new group that it's better for them to send material to *NME, Music Week* and *Sounds*. They have more space to fill, and reach a more street-level readership.

'Bands have got to have made more inroads than just being brand-new for *No.1*. They really need to have had two or three records out, usually.'

So canvass your outlets carefully. It is a complete waste of time sending out information to every single one, and targeting your attack should make all the difference. Time spent poring over magazines and papers, watching television programmes and listening to the radio will be well worth it.

NATIONAL NEWSPAPERS

The national papers very rarely cover new groups – unless there is an amazing story to tell. But very occasionally they will run talent competitions, so do not ignore them completely: just keep your eyes and ears peeled.

The *Star*, for example, is not a paper to waste your money on when unknown. Rick Sky reveals: 'The *Star* is very hooked on chart bands. We do predictions, but these are made with a look at the charts. It is not really worth new bands getting in touch. I am also very wary of unknown bands. It's usually a load of hype, with no story. It's amazing to what extremes bands – or their managers – will go to to get some publicity. No matter how powerful the media and general press hype may be, bands have to have good music.'

John Blake, who has a daily pop column in the *Daily Mirror*, has been watching the music business for years. He explains his policy: 'Although I have a huge respect for new talent, we don't write about new groups very often because our readership demands stories about established artists.

'We are definitely in a dead cycle at the moment. The music business is just wallowing around, record sales are falling and A & Rs are more interested in signing bands with a tried and tested formula than anything new and different.

'The music business gets like this every ten years or so, but this time around it is different. It is interesting to note that the population of the country is older. There are now fewer teenagers, more people in their twenties and thirties. Therefore the long-standing artists are still popular, especially on CDs: Phil Collins, Dire Straits, for example. More AOR [adult-oriented rock] records are being sold than ever before. It therefore makes it harder for new bands.

'Last year there was not one million-selling platinum single. The best-selling single was the *EastEnders* one – what a joke!

'It is difficult for a band to be long-lasting nowadays because there is so much media attention. When I started my pop column on the *Evening News* ten to eleven years ago it was fairly easy for bands to build up a grass-roots following and develop slowly. Now there are so many rock shows and music columns that anything of interest is picked up immediately. Bands can get blasted out of all recognition before they have even started.

'Although we rarely mention new groups, we have organized a talent competition this year and I have been amazed at the number of tapes sent in – about 6000. It just shows how many people are out there trying to get into the business. Although many of the tapes are dross, some are very good. Billy Gaff has promised to put in £¼ million for the winner, which should make him, her or them a star.'

So it all comes down to you doing your homework. By reading the particular publication you think you might be able to interest, you will soon be able to establish whether new bands are something it covers or not.

The 'Ad Lib' section of the *London Evening Standard* is a good target for new artists. Peter Holt, Ad Lib's editor, says: 'We are very keen on writing about new bands. We have given publicity to many unknown bands over the years. We wrote about Madonna six months before anyone else.

'We'll write about bands before they're signed, if there's a story or angle to write about. We've certainly helped bands to get a record deal – or at least been instrumental in their success.'

TELEVISION

Find out which radio and television programmes use and cover new music, check out which one fits your sort of music and try it.

It is important to work out – before you contact the programme-makers and possibly blow it by sending the wrong material – what sort of music they are looking for, whom to contact and how. To do this, either watch the programme and check the credits at the end (you are looking for the producer's name) or telephone the programme. Ask to speak to the producer, and whoever is on duty will come to the phone, if free. Remember, just as you want to get on the programme, no one wants to miss out on something which might be the next Frankie Goes to Hollywood or Duran Duran. If the producer is prepared to give you a few minutes, have a chat, but be as succinct as possible.

Each programme has its preferences regarding how it is approached. The producer of *Whistle Test* explains: 'We do use unsigned bands. The band should find out the name of the producer first and send a cassette to him. They must be interesting and look right for *Whistle Test*. We will see them live first, so they should send two or three songs, photographs and a list of gigs. If they send a stamped addressed envelope it will force people to reply.

'As a general rule, we are unlikely to book someone we couldn't go to see. In the old days we used to audition groups, but there's no money for that now.'

The Tube also uses both signed and unsigned bands. A researcher reveals: 'We like to discover people. We see ourselves as a little A & R outfit.'

It is not interested in receiving anything more than a demo tape. 'There is so much paper, we are quite happy not to have anything more; that means a bio and picture are not necessary. The simpler it is the better. Music is the core, and we will never put on a band without seeing them live first. We'll see them in rehearsal rooms if they have no gigs, but it is far less embarrassing for both sides if we see a live performance.

'Any act can have a go, but a new band has to be really good and worth presenting. We veer away from middle-of-the-road stuff. We like more pioneering or exciting music.'

Children's programmes can be a good outlet, but remember the emphasis is on kids and therefore your music must be appropriate.

The *Wide Awake Club* on TV AM, for example, occasionally uses new music. This is aimed at 6- to 12-year-olds, although it does have a wider audience, so your music must have the right content for the show.

As the programme's producer observes: 'The pop content is quite small. We only use two pop items in the 2-hour show. Basically the music must be bright, up-tempo and danceable.

'We get tapes from new groups sent to us via managers, record shops, etc. and we have used unsigned groups. We will listen to tapes, demos and rough videos. The worst thing for us is being sent a whole load of tapes by a music company which is full of the wrong stuff – heavy metal, for instance. In the pile there might well be a couple of great tapes, but we have to find them.

'At the moment we can't use videos. We have had facilities to shoot short videos in the past. We would take

3 hours to shoot a 3-minute video. Then the group could buy it if they wanted, but the cost would probably be prohibitive.'

Look out for any competitions the Saturday-morning children's shows might be running. *Saturday Superstore* is running a talent contest for 16-17-year-old groups for the third year running.

One of the programme's producers recalls: 'Last year, the baby pop group that won was really good. We very, very occasionally use groups who have no record label, but the trouble with them is that they are mostly too untogether. The last time we wanted to use a new group, it took such a long time to arrange that the leader of the group left before we got them into the studio. Time is vitally important.'

Again, not only must you be professional in your first approach, but if you do get interest it is vital that you rehearse until you are note-perfect. All studio time costs money and any programmes – whether television or radio – ideally want a band to go into the studio, record and get out again – fast.

Every programme has a limited budget and has to bear its audience in mind. On the whole viewers want to see big bands, people whom they know. 'If a group had a big buzz,' says *Saturday Superstore*, 'and is really good, we might not care. We did that with Howard Jones. And we were the first TV programme to put on Wham! and A-Ha. We have to pay the MU minimum so, for example, we will be forking out roughly £600-£700 for a six- or seven-piece band. If a group is really together and excellent, we might give them a chance, in which case it would be worth their contacting the programme and sending a cassette. But you've got to remember that we can always get a really good group for the same money as an amateurish one.'

RADIO

Some might say Britain is unfortunate in having only one national radio channel. Because the charts are so important, the competition for radio play has given Radio 1 tremendous power, which has inevitably led to unethical attempts to get records broadcast. It is human nature.

The days of payola and large-scale hyping of the charts may have disappeared but it cannot be denied – although many will try to do so – that bribery occurs.

Where do you draw the line? Offering valuable gifts, money or drugs is not acceptable, but does taking a producer of one of the main daytime, record-selling shows out to lunch count?

Radio 1 air-time is divided into day and night. Daytime shows run from 5.30 a.m. to 7.30 p.m. and are based on a playlist (described in Chapter 11), which broadly means that the records you hear are mostly from the top forty. It does not leave much room for new records or unknown groups. But the situation is improving. When Johnny Beerling took over as Radio 1 controller he instigated a policy change that enabled listeners to hear a non-established artist every half-hour.

Roger Lewis, the *Simon Bates* producer, says: 'We didn't play punk at the time it happened, but if it happened now we would do so. We play more rock, too: we even play Iron Maiden. People still think that Simon Bates plays exclusively top forty tracks. In fact he regularly plays some records in the lower half of the charts and one or two which are not in the charts at all. One day, for example, we played Glass Tiger – a new band and one Radio 1 has championed. We played the record for eight weeks running.

'We have played a single from the Bible twice now [in 1986] – they are a new band on a small record label. I chose their record from the normal huge pile of records because I liked it. It got nowhere. They released a second single, we played that – and now they've got themselves a plugger. But we played it because it was a good song. My main criterion is that a record will sound good on radio.'

Night-time Radio 1, which runs from 7.30 p.m., is not playlisted. This gives shows the freedom to play what they wish. The style of music played becomes radically different, so you find shows such as *Janice Long, Andy Kershaw* and *John Peel* playing new bands and little of the chart stuff. But plays at this time do not sell the same quantity of records as daytime play. What they do do is to give your band exposure.

Janice Long's show acts as a bridge between the day- and night-time shows. She plays a mixture of interesting known and unknown bands. On *Peel* you will find far more off-the-wall, experimental music.

Mike Hawkes, Janice's producer, describes what they are looking for: 'We offer an alternative to what is played during the day, and we try to encourage new bands, but no heavy metal or MOR. We are only interested in records and doing sessions. Occasionally we will use unsigned bands.

'We do get sent mountains of demo tapes, but they just end up in the cupboard – I can't do anything with them. I wish I *did* have the time to listen to everything sent in. Sometimes I'll listen to them in the car to and from work. If a group is recommended to me, then that is a different matter. We do two sessions a week.'

Anne Nightingale will only play records. If she is sent demo tapes, she passes them on to Janice or John Peel.

John Peel's show is still one of the best to approach as a new band – if you are unusual, different and good. John Walters has been producing Peel's show for an amazing twenty years. They are like an old married couple to talk to – not surprising, perhaps, as they have been together so long. During Walters' interview for this book, Peel breezed in and they spent five minutes arguing over who had last seen the toothpaste-squeezer. And this was in their tiny Radio 1 office, full to the ceiling with boxes of records and tapes, at 12 noon.

Walters sees their programme as 'the dipstick of where the energy is'. They are mostly concerned with the sound, and the first 30 seconds of any tape count the most. It is no good sending a tape in, then ringing up a week later saying you've got some better songs, and would they be interested? What you send must be right first time.

Peel and Walters are not interested in pictures, biographies, stories or people trying to come in to talk to them. If the tape or record doesn't grab their attention, that's it. So pick out one song which stands out – think of it as a trailer for a film. Remember that you have to make an impression that eclipses all the rest, including continual interruptions such as phones ringing and people popping in and out.

Walters recalls: 'When we started it was much easier. We had one programme a week and used to be really on the case. We worked through the new labels, such as Island, who would tip us off about a band and we'd go to see them. Bands didn't have access to recording in those days; they had to be seen to be picked up by a record company.

'I remember a handsome face appearing round the door one day, saying "I knew you from Newcastle, saw you play in a jazz group." We chatted a bit, he left a tape of his band and I listened to it a bit later. We went to check out the band – total unknowns – who were playing in Wimbledon, and then played them. His name was Brian Ferry, and the band Roxy Music. That just doesn't happen nowadays – there's just no time to check out the new acts.

'We get absolutely inundated with tapes and records now. And it's a really depressing job listening to them all. There are so many uninteresting ones. You can listen to 50 and hear only one that is vaguely interesting. Peel selects on an instinctive basis.'

Peel butts in: 'I'm not interested in the singing, I just have to like the feel of the thing. I listen to most of the tapes when I have to drive long distances. I take hundreds with me and come back with only four worth listening to.'

If you want to get a session on the *Peel* show, all you need to send is an idea of what you sound like. Walters and Peel are both so experienced that they can easily hear if something is going to be worth recording. If you *do* get the chance of a *Peel* session, make sure you are well rehearsed. Remember, it is not a workshop and time-wasting is not appreciated. You can do that in a commercial studio, when *you* are paying for it.

Capital Radio is the other main outlet to aim for. Although it is not national, it has an important place in the music business and, of course, broadcasts the Network charts along with all the other independent radio stations, and a few foreign ones, on Sunday afternoons.

Capital tends to reflect more of what is happening in London. Records that are big on the London disco or hip-hop scene might get played, even though they are not big nationally and would probably not be touched by

Radio 1; and Capital does try to keep an ear to the ground, several disc jockeys spending time in the clubs and pubs in the evenings.

Jon Myer, executive producer of Capital, says: 'We listen to everything that gets sent in, whether it be on a new label or Elton John. Both are treated in the same way – on their musical merit – but naturally you cannot ignore a new Elton John single. If it's a good record it should be heard.

'If you don't have a record, you can get on Capital by doing live or pre-recorded sessions. Send a demo tape in, but make sure it is sent to the right slot.'

Sara Ward has been working for Capital for some time, doing interviews with groups, and also hosting a weekly pop programme on the BBC World Service. This is what she looks for: 'Groups send in tapes and if they are any good, with an interesting story for an interview, we will play it. I look for something that will catch the ear. I like commercial stuff if it is well produced. But I'm mostly interested in voices.

'I like to receive a tape with a good biography and a friendly, informal letter. It must be interesting – a good angle to talk about is vital. I love the idea that someone has bothered to send it in. It doesn't matter if they haven't a record deal, as long as they have made an effort. If they have sent a good letter, I will take the time to listen to the tape carefully.

'The way a band promotes itself is very important. When sending in info, don't make silly mistakes, like spelling: it shows you don't care enough, you're not trying to make an impression. Don't just give basic information. We must get a spontaneous feeling about a group. You can tell five minutes before an interview if you are going to get something out of it. Groups need original ideas – perhaps they have put out a special EP, have a different background, something others haven't, so there is an angle for people to talk or write about. The Nightingales, for example, did a whole lot of seaside gigs last summer. They were fresh and funny, using all old summery numbers. Great!

'Ideally I like three songs, especially if they are different, so I get a good range, but two will do. It's useful for the band to be gigging so we can check it out.

'The band has got to be able to talk. They must work out little anecdotes to make a good interview. Before a band comes in, it should take time to think about it. They need to be lively. Icicle Works, for example, were good to interview. They were really funny and had good stories.

'When doing interviews I like groups who come in and know how and what to put across, give an insight into their personalities. Groups should find out about the programmes they are going on to . . . what that person likes.'

If you should get the chance of doing a programme which includes an interview and your band has quite a few members, work out beforehand who is going to be spokesman, or in what order you are going to speak. And remember, an interview should be fun. Don't think of it as 'us' and 'them'. You may not be singing or playing, but you're still supposed to be providing entertainment.

Finally, don't forget local radio – both the station in the area where you are based and those in the towns where you hope to have gigs.

CHAPTER 14

Videos

Since Queen's first, spectacular video, 'Bohemian Rhapsody' in the early 1970s, the video industry has never looked back. Videos have steadily increased in importance, perhaps reaching their zenith in the early 'eighties. Although no longer overridingly essential to a group's success, they will never go away.

Jonathan King comments: 'As an observer, I would say that for the last six years the thing has been for artists to be visual. Over the next four years, I think the focus will return to music. The visual aspect has not been the best thing for music.'

But it is undeniable that videos have altered the face of the music business, especially in the context of playing live. As an eminent manager says: 'The difference between now and the 'sixties is that we live in a video age. It used to take ages before a band was big enough and well-known enough to play huge stadiums, especially in America. With videos, you can have a relatively new band playing to millions of front rooms, which has the same effect as playing round all the circuits. A video makes the band larger than life. A couple of hit singles and an album will give you a sell-out concert at Wembley. You couldn't do that before.'

Videos are just another marketing tool, necessary for increasing the public's awareness of a group and its record. But the sound will always be more important than the picture. The song must take priority. Although a stunning video might enhance its initial impact, it is the song which will be remembered, except in a very few and very exceptional cases.

Some record companies are very much against videos – after all, they are another marketing cost to be budgeted for

– but artists, not surprisingly, are keen to make them. Therefore, rather than making videos for each new single, record companies now concentrate on two different types: the ones made for big star groups, for which no expense is spared, and the others for the groups which the company has decided to promote heavily. Because videos are so expensive record companies often prefer to wait until they know a record is selling before they make one. It is easy to spend more money on the video than on the production of a record. If, say, the total budget is £50,000, the company might cut its recording budget in order to produce a video, to the detriment of the record.

The problem with not making a video at the outset is that one of the best ways to get a single publicity, especially with newer bands, is television exposure, and for that you need a video.

In one record company managing director's opinion, 'They are an unnecessary evil. I wish they'd never been invented. Very few enhance a song. They are just one further thing that puts the business in the hands of people making money. But you have to do it, to keep up.'

Another managing director admits: 'We are not very good at making videos as an industry yet. Even MTV, the American video channel, is boring because the videos are so boring. There are only a few very good ones – and those stick out a mile and sell records.'

On the other hand, videos can save time for the artists. That television exposure, if achieved, will build them far more quickly than weeks spent on the road touring. New bands can do cheap videos if they can get an original idea – a great one was made by Fuzzbox in 1986 for just a few hundred pounds.

Professionally-made videos are very expensive. The rock-bottom price now for a good video is £8000. Dr & the Medics last video cost only £5000 because they pulled in favours: many people involved in the video were contributing their services for no fee (even so, the true cost would only have been £10,000, which is still low).

The expense lies not so much in the actual film but in the labour, because of union rates and regulations over the number of technicians required. The content and location of the video will also affect its cost.

It is more difficult now than it was a few years ago to make a professional video on the cheap because production companies are less keen to work for a low fee. Record companies have asked them too often to do a cheap video on the promise of a more lucrative one later, but then they are asked to do another favour, and another.

One video director reveals: 'Lots of record companies will collect ideas from a number of different video companies, then go nowhere with them. They ask for ideas, story-boards, our time... but we are paid nothing. One video company was given 90 scripts to work on, but only 5 came through.

'Videos will never end: as long as people watch the box, there will be videos.'

If your record company talks about making an extravagant video, using an expensive producer in an exotic location, think about it. It might sound wonderful – good for your image and fun to do, although it will probably be harder work than you imagine – but remember the cost is *recoupable*, from you: how much of it depends on your contract, but it is highly likely to be the entire amount. It is up to you to work out, with your manager and record company, the value of making such a video. Weigh up the possibility of increased sales against the cost of the film. Of course, a brilliant video does not ensure television coverage, and even if you get that, it will not ensure sales of your record, although it should certainly increase them.

You can never guarantee how the video will turn out, either, however much you spend on it. Videos made to promote a single have a very short life – many are made, at huge cost, and never even shown. One Janet Jackson video, for one of her 1986 singles, purportedly cost £250,000, yet the single had only a month's life.

Beware of record companies which try to bamboozle you into using an expensive in-vogue producer. They might say: 'Go to Joe Bloggs. He's done brilliant things. It'll cost £40,000.' Remember, you'll be tenth on his list of importance, and that the money is recoupable from you. Talk to people, find out who does videos you like, suggest to your record company whom you would like and say why.

Often a simpler, cheaper video can be far more effective than a clever-clever one, full of special effects which detract from the music rather than enhancing it. There is quite an art – which sadly is not often in evidence, as yet – in producing a video which truly complements a song.

Recently it has become more and more usual for a manager and new group to pay for their own video, in order to have control over the director and the expense, and at least to ensure the cost will not have to come off royalties.

When making a video with a production company, do not be surprised if you find you have very little say in what is going on. If you feel strongly about how it should go, make sure you make the point before the actual day of filming arrives. If not, you may well find the record company's A & R people order you and the video producer around – though very often, when the band hasn't a clue what it is doing, this is the best way of working. So when you sign a video contract, watch out for how much or little control you have over the video.

One video director describes how he works: 'I much prefer to meet the bands first and throw ideas round and deal with them direct. After all, the video is meant to be for and about them.'

Home videos for promotional use for A & Rs, publishers, managers and the media are a different matter. A cheaply made home video can be a useful tool, ingraining your name over those of other bands in their minds, and on this level videos are less expensive to make.

One music journalist, for example, says: 'I will always look at videos sent in, and if they look interesting, follow the band up.'

If a group feels at a disadvantage from being out of town, it might get more interest from A & R people if they have seen a video first. If they like the band, then they might pay to go up to see it, or invite it down. It just might give that band a bit of an edge. But the music still has to be good.

Jill Sinclair, the producer of *The Chart Show*, says she

will always look at home-produced videos. 'If the group sends a tape to the programme, we will chart its progress and might talk about it to an agent or manager. But the video must be of broadcastable quality. One big mistake groups make is to save up a few hundred pounds to make a video, do it well but don't realize they have to be members of MU. Then everything is wasted, because we can't use it.

'We don't need to deal with a record company, but we do need tour dates, or some means of the public buying, seeing or hearing them. It's no use otherwise. It's no good expecting television to work in isolation: you must think of it as just one part of media promotion as a whole.

'The sort of video I am looking for must be original, or have a sense of humour, or be infectious, memorable, entertaining.'

If groups have no money and want to make a video, there are two ways in which they might be able to enlist some help. Most towns have film and video workshops which are sponsored by the government. The workshops are responsible for local video production and have a moral duty to help local groups. You might be able to persuade them to help, if the video is concerned with the locality. The video workshops are funded by the British Film Institute (see page 178), which produces a yearbook listing all of them.

Secondly, most towns have art colleges with technical facilities for video-making. You may well have friends at the college who can help and if you approach the right people tactfully they might be able to do something for you at a cheap rate. But you must be prepared to work late or start, for example, at 6 a.m. on a Sunday morning, and return the equipment in time for the next lecture. It will give the students some practical experience and you should be able to work out a satisfactory deal with them. With friends filming, your video could cost as little as £200 – but it's a huge risk to make one that way, especially if you are unsure of their filming abilities.

Once the video is made, it will not cost a great deal to make VHS copies, which you can send out – clearly marked, and with a concise covering letter.

Here are a couple of tips for making d-i-y videos: the simpler the video, the better, but use your imagination; and stick to one location – it is cheaper and will save time (a 3-minute video will take about a day to film, so the last thing you want to do is to spend too much time moving around). Also, make sure the first thing you do is to cover the entire song two or three times. Then, even if everything goes disastrously wrong, at least you will have something to use. You nearly always have to mime, and this puts many bands out, if they are not used to doing it. So practise first.

There are two basic types of pop video: the straight performance (you can't really go wrong with that and it is the cheapest option) and the 'creative' sort. If you opt for the latter, keep it simple: play safe and don't be too clever. Remember to keep a sense of humour; people have to like the video and you're on it, so be likeable.

Before you start making your own video, watch loads of other videos, get an idea of how you want yours to go, but don't copy somebody else's ideas too closely.

If you are not good in front of the camera, don't attempt to be the front man: it will be very noticeable. But if you *can* flirt with the camera, do it. Try a few shots first. Don't be too ambitious.

You must also be aware of the IBA guidelines. If you are not sure about them, ring up the IBA and have them sent to you. There are rules to be followed on sex, smoking, gratuitous violence, advertising, etc. Smoking is OK after 9.00 in the evening, but is not allowed in a kids' programme. So when making a video which you think might go well on a Saturday-morning television programme, for example, don't submit something which shows smoking. It will not be used, however good the video is otherwise. And you must keep within the law: for example, no shots of driving a car without a seat-belt or while drinking, or of riding a motorbike with no helmet.

Be aware of peripheral traps: avoid activities such as bull-fighting or other forms of cruelty to animals. Advertising is another point to watch. For example, don't film in front of a well-known hamburger joint, or show a coke can too clearly. Names on guitars are considered OK.

Videos for television use have to be of broadcastable quality and made with suitable equipment on high-quality tape. On the whole a video made on low-band tape, the sort used for home movies, is not acceptable.

The chief quality controller at the IBA explains: 'Quality is the most important thing. Certain television channels like to keep the quality of their films high. For example, Thames TV does not want to be put in the category of cable TV. But the quality of most pop videos is OK.

'For those you can use 16mm film, but basically it is only as good as the people who use it. If you have an amateur cameraman using the best-quality gear, you will still get unbroadcastable tape.

'ITV companies and Channel 4 are required to meet certain standards. At the moment C-format 1-inch machines and Beta Cam, which was originally intended as a replacement for 16mm for news items, provide good, impressive quality. In theory, the latter should not be of broadcastable quality, but in many instances it is quite acceptable.

'Technological advances are happening constantly at the moment. Things are always changing. Tomorrow there will be something called M2. Quality rather than the actual type of tape is the key.'

It has been known for a band to make its video on Super 8, but videos made on this have to be transferred on to proper tape for television. Fuzzbox, for example, used Super 8 for one of their first videos. The difference was easily noticeable, but you could argue that that was the effect they wanted.

CHAPTER 15

Doing it all yourself

It is possible to sidestep record and production companies altogether by putting out your own record, getting it pressed and distributed, and sending it to radio and television programmes to get it publicized.

The first thing you will need if you are going it alone is the industry bible, *The Music Week Directory* (see page 179). This lists all the names and addresses you may want from studios and sleeve designers to pluggers and distribution companies.

Going it alone is one way to bring yourself to the notice of record companies, publishers, producers, managers and so on if you have not been able to generate enough interest through gigging.

The Icicle Works, for example, chose this route: 'We decided to put out our own single because we felt that that way at least we could get some product out. We recorded a 7-inch single with three tracks at a local studio. It was very rough; we still hadn't really decided on our style. It was distributed by Probe Records, who are Liverpool-based, to the Cartel [a group of independent distributors]. We sold about 2000 copies and got on to the independent charts. It helped us to get a deal. So did the session we did for John Peel.

'Recording, cutting, pressing, sleeve artwork, travel, etc. cost about £1200. One of the group put in £200. Our manager, Tony Barwood, paid the rest. We did deals all round, pulled in as many favours as we could. We used a local art guy who we knew had done good stuff: he charged only £50 as opposed to £200.

'Tony did most of the plugging. He went down to London and hung around Radio 1 until he got his appointments. He managed to get quite a few plays. We did have problems with wholesalers not stocking it. In the end he had to ring all the independent members of the Cartel to check what was happening. We eventually got to no. 10 in the Independent chart.

'It definitely got the band more notice, and then attracted the attention of the publishers – Chappell – who liked the idea of three tracks on the one record. They rang up and said they wanted to pick up the publishing of that single. No money was offered, but they said they would help us work it.

'Eventually we did a proper deal with Chappell. And the advance was sufficient to enable us to record another independent single. This time we could afford a better producer and a decent studio. Chappell paid for marketing, and a plugger. We made a good video, which was not broadcastable but was useful for the plugger.

'The second single was distributed by Beggars' Banquet and pressed by them. It was just a one-off deal. This time the single got to no. 2 in the independent charts and 97 in the main chart.'

So it can be done, if you have some idea of where to go and what to do, and you could end up with a one-off deal with a publisher or independent record company enabling you to produce an even better record. But you must have an idea of how to publicize and push the record, to make it worthwhile from your point of view and the distributor's, who will need to be convinced that his bills will be paid.

Think carefully about which tracks you put on your single. You are aiming to increase exposure of your band and sell your record and the best way to do that is to get radio play – local, regional and national. So the track must be one that sounds good over the airwaves, which may be very different to one that goes down well live. You must choose the strongest track – a good, original song with impact and one that has some memorable qualities.

Your record must capture people's imaginations. The act of buying a piece of plastic is an emotional gesture. You must be able to play and produce music people can relate to.

After recording the chosen two or three tracks you will need to have a lacquer cut from the ¼-inch master tape.

This is done at a cutting room, lists of which are in the *Music Week Directory*; otherwise the studio will probably advise you. The soundwaves from your tape are cut mechanically into grooves in a lacquer – an aluminium disc coated with plasticky material. The depth and width of each groove varies according to the sound pattern emitted by your tape.

Some pressing plants will need to be given a lacquer; others will work from the master tape. When the lacquer reaches the factory it will have metal 'grown' on to it to make a 'positive', which has grooves, from which a 'negative' is grown which has ridges: this is known as the 'stamper', from which the records are pressed.

The stamper goes up on the press with the customer's label. The minimum quantity of records pressed is usually 1000, but some plants will press as few as 500. The smaller the quantity, the more expensive each individual record will be.

If you decide you want to issue your own record, you will have to decide on a label name. Before you give this name, and a catalogue number, to the pressing company, check with Gallup (see page 178) that the name and catalogue number you have chosen do not already exist. Otherwise you will have problems with sales records, especially if your single should enter the charts.

It is unnecessary nowadays to form a record company, although if you wish to do this you should be able to buy a company off the shelf for about £150. Ask your accountant and lawyer about the advantages and disadvantages of doing so.

Today, you are looking at a cost of about £600-£1000 for pressing, artwork, labelling and bagging for a thousand 7-inch records. To keep costs down you could opt for a plain white sleeve, which would save you £200-£500: these are perfectly acceptable to radio and television programmes and the music press, and are OK for selling in the shops too. If people like your music they will buy the record regardless of whether or not it has a picture or a plain sleeve. But if the record should get into the top fifty, when the public *really* starts buying, the chances are that, given a choice between two similar records, it will go for the one in a picture bag.

In addition to your production costs you will have to pay for recording. Recording studios outside London are cheaper than those in the capital, but check out what the studio offers – the sound quality and the capabilities of the engineer, in particular. You can get the single pressed either by a local company – as Icicle Works did – or give the master tape to a London outfit.

The better you are at wheeling and dealing, the cheaper it will be. You can either deal with each bit of the processing yourself, but this is time-consuming and you will need to be very organized to do it, or you can get a company to deal with the whole process for you. Again, contacts help.

Any pressing company dealing with a new client would want the money up front, 50 per cent payable with the order, and if the rest is paid in cash you can take the product away immediately. You should hope for a 5-working-day turnround. Speak to lots of pressing companies: it is possible you can make a deal for one to distribute as well for you.

Pressing companies all work slightly differently. One, for example, will take a ¼-inch master, get the lacquer cut, and if the band scribbles down a rough design, develop a label. That will take 7-10 days, depending mainly on artwork. But if the pressing plant is currently busy pressing thousands of copies of a hit single, be prepared for delays. Check first.

Expect the following average charges (correct at the time of going to press) for 1000 albums: labels, 2p each; processing from ¼-inch to lacquer, £47.50 per side; lacquer to stamper, £37.50 per side; pressing, about 38p per record. Sleeves could cost about 17p each per 1000, with plate changes about £95 each.

If you can first find a distributor who is interested in your single, this can be advantageous as it may well be able to develop the artwork and decide which pressing company to go through (and should get better rates). But you will need to have generated a buzz about your group and built up quite a bit of local interest before the distributing company will consider taking on your record.

It is essential to sort out distribution. It's all very well to have boxes of singles piled up and the record being played on the radio, but if you can't get the records into the shops you might as well not have bothered.

Be prepared to take a lot of time finding the right distributor. First, check out who distributes records of a similar sort to yours. Go to several companies and see what sort of deal you can get.

The distribution company should be firmly committed to your single: it has to make its sales reps enthusiastic, so that they can sell it into the shops, and be convinced that you have the know-how to promote and pay for the record.

It is not nearly as easy nowadays as it was four or five years ago to press a thousand records and persuade a distribution company to take them on. So many companies have suffered as a result of broken promises that they are far more careful now. Rough Trade, for instance, no longer takes on records from individual bands; it prefers to deal with proven labels. But the other members of the Cartel will still do one-off deals.

The Cartel is a network of six independent distribution companies dotted around Britain – York, Leamington Spa, Norwich, Bristol, Edinburgh and Rough Trade in London. If one of the out-of-London members is approached for a one-off deal, it will either take, for example, a thousand records on a consignment basis, accounting for their sales monthly and charging a distribution fee of about 28 per cent of dealer price; or, if convinced that you will be able to pay for the manufacturing cost, it might take on both manufacturing and distribution.

However, do not be dispirited if one or more distributors turn your single down. Just because they don't like it, it doesn't mean to say the single is no good. Persevere.

The London firm PRT, one of the largest pressing and distribution companies, works on the following premise. A band sends in a tape or cassette. It is presented at one of PRT's regular meetings and if it is not liked overall it is rejected. (A couple of years ago, the picture was different: the company took anything and everything, but it lost out on so many dismal records that this practice was stopped.)

If the record is OK, PRT meets representatives from the

label (the band, if it is acting as its own record company), fundamentally to check out its viability, and also its ability to market it, pay for a plugger, and so on. PRT's attitude is that radio is so important that if the record company can't get or can't afford to push the producers to take it, it is not worth its own while to press and distribute it.

A representative of PRT explains: 'The problem with small labels is that although they can usually afford studio costs, cutting and manufacturing, they can't pay for the rest. If they cannot pay or have no idea of how to push the single it will just be lost in the mêlée of all the other records coming out.'

PRT's manufacturing costs are currently 15½p for a 7-inch record, 33p for a 12-inch. The distribution percentage ranges from 25 to 28. The minimum number of records is 2000 for a 7-inch, 1000 for a 12-inch. For disco records, the reverse is the case: the minimum is 1000 7-inches, 2000 12-inches.

PRT needs labels and sleeves supplied. Try to find a graphic designer who will work for you as cheaply as possible. If you are on a tight budget, go for a white sleeve (or any other single colour) for the first few thousand. Then, if the record is selling, you can decide if you want picture bags for the next lot you have pressed up (see below).

If you decide on a colour sleeve, it is important to have one that stands out. Working with more than two colours will be much more expensive. So go for a simple but striking design.

One graphic designer who has been involved with label design for eight years comments: 'Sleeves are very important. There has always been a conflict between the designer's concept of visual image and what the record company thinks. The designer has to look at the group as a product and work on its identity. I like to meet with the band and see them play. If the band wants to put forward ideas, which they usually do, they should look at record sleeves and find something they particularly like. They could contact the designer (the record company can usually provide the number), to see what else he has done and go from there.

'It is most dangerous to design a sleeve which is high fashion when the band isn't. Also it will go out of style more quickly. You should never go for something the band can't live up to.'

Another way of doing things is to go to one of the several companies who will organize the whole thing for you. They will take either a ¼-inch master tape and ideas for artwork, or the lacquer and finished artwork, and deliver the completed product to your door. They can also arrange distribution and take much of the organization off your shoulders. Although this might sound a more expensive way of doing things, it does not necessarily work out so. It could save you a lot of time and aggro, and because they are dealing with pressing companies, designers and so on all the time they will be able to get a better deal than you would ever be able to.

The managing director of one of these companies outlines the advantages: 'Instead of a small label having to deal with many different companies, it can pay one person to look after the whole thing. That saves time and hassle.

'We are able to offer good rates because we are dealing with large orders. If a small company wanted a few thousand labels, it would cost them far more per unit than if they could order half a million.

'With new clients we will ask for all the money up front. If they give us a ¼-inch master and artwork ideas we will transform that into a package.

'Five hundred singles would cost around £600. We like to be able to give clients the finished product within three weeks, throughout the year.'

A representative of another company explains: 'A small label can come in with a tape and we will do the whole lot. We have our own design team and will organize artwork, sleeves, labels, manufacturing, photo sessions, and so on. Price varies enormously depending on the artwork etc. We can work from black and white pictures or colour trannies. If you are on a low budget we will suggest how to keep costs down as much as possible. A thousand records is the minimum.'

Think carefully about when you release your record: it is

important to get the timing right. Summer is notoriously bad, but if you leave it too late you will get caught up with the flood of Christmas releases. You may put out a record in October and start to do well. Then the Christmas records will hit the market and knock out everything else.

The volume of products produced and the air-time available will never be equal and it gets worse all the time. The record industry launches new products every day, and inevitably much disappears without trace.

Another problem that might arise is that you could start making an impression on the charts, then a major artist releases his new single and drives your record out. So keep your ears to the ground and be aware of what else is going on.

In 1986 4474 singles were released, an average of 86 per week; and 5050 albums, averaging 97 a week. Fifty per cent of the singles sales occur in the top twenty, so there's only another 50 per cent left for all the other records, including the newest bands trying to creep into the charts at 200.

The level of sales needed for a record to reach the charts differs depending on the time of year. In the summer you might enter the lower end of the charts with 500 sales (near Christmas it could take 10,000). To get into the top 75 you'll need to sell a minimum of 2000 records.

A successful band's no. 1 single in the UK could sell between 500,000 and 1,000,000 copies; a no. 10, 200,000.

Although the distributor should place your record in as many record shops as it can – and its knowledge of where and whom to approach will be better than yours – there is nothing to stop you approaching your local record shop, which should be happy to take your single if you have worked up a local following.

The major retailers concentrate on chart records, but the smaller record shops (there are about 60-70 independent ones in Britain) are far more geared to the independent scene.

The Probe shop in Liverpool, for instance, stocks virtually everything on the independent scene. Its manager explains: 'We take nothing that is too commercial, and never stock all the chart stuff. We stock a lot of local groups' records – mainly from Liverpool, some from Manchester. Groups come in and say, "Will you sell our records?" And we will if they are any good. We take the records on sale or return, so we have nothing to lose and it is helping the local groups.

'We'll also take a tape from a local group and if it's good we'll press up a few thousand for them. We'll sell the records in the shop and give them the rest to sell at gigs, etc.'

Sadly, the number of independent record shops is diminishing – mainly because the major ones are expanding voraciously, buying up the smaller chains. The independent shops also lose out because the record industry will sell to anyone and the small shops find it hard to compete with the discounts the multiples can offer the public.

The owner of Andy's Record Stores, an independent chain with nine branches in the south-east, says: 'We have a feel for the market, we know what our customers want and what is selling. I take a pride in that. All our staff know what they are talking about, unlike most shops 10 miles out of London.

'Sometimes we stock local bands who have pressed a thousand of their own record, on a sale or return basis.'

You could advertise your record cheaply by flyposting, but be aware of the problems. You might dream of papering the Western Hemisphere, but it's actually rather more difficult than you think, especially in London. Firstly, flyposting is a civil offence. You might be moved on by the police, although the only people who actually have grounds for taking you to court are the owners of the site you are defacing. Secondly, little mafias spring up who will tear down, or cover up, your poster within a day or two. Sometimes they will be ripped down by the following morning. Some bands will pay up to £6000 to have a poster project done well.

Posters are good for the band's egos, and people do buy because of them, especially if a buzz has been generated about the band. Posters help to create a sense of something happening.

Once you have a release date for your record you should aim to get as much press as possible. The national press is unlikely to be interested, but your local papers should be and the music papers which review singles should be sent a copy of the record. Try to get the attention of a local journalist. Good music is not necessarily enough on its own: it helps to have a striking, original picture and an angle or story for the journalist to write about too.

Be as professional as possible in your approach. Write neat letters, check your spelling and be concise. Put your name, address and telephone number on the letter and the record, and provide a biography if you can see this might be useful.

If you have had just 500 or 1000 records pressed, you will want to give away as few as possible, so it is vital to work out exactly where to target your product.

First, buy every music paper and magazine for at least two weeks and read them thoroughly. Work out which section you need to send your record to – the singles review editor (use his or her name if the column regularly carries the same byline) or someone who writes about your sort of music. If you send it just to the publication, it is likely to get lost.

Giving the name of an individual as part of the address saves time when your record reaches the publication's offices and makes sure that it will be (or at least should be) heard. Never forget that you are fighting against the other hundred singles released every week. Sending your record to a magazine does not, of course, guarantee a review. However, it will do no harm to ring the addressee about a week later just to check he or she has received it. In all likelihood he will have done, but telephoning gives you a chance to jog his memory, have a quick chat to reinforce your name in his mind and ask, at the end of the conversation, whether he might be reviewing your record or not. If you get a good reaction – maybe he has already listened to and is enthusiastic about your track – keep an eye on the review section and if it is not mentioned that week ring up again to find out what happened.

A gentle nudge does no harm; being over-pushy (e.g.

ringing up every day) is another matter. And be prepared for the writer to be off-hand, short or downright sharp because he has an editor over his shoulder screaming for copy he should have produced two hours earlier. If this happens, just ring off and ring back later. The more contact you make, the more likely it is that your name will be put slightly higher on the writer's mental checklist than that of someone who has had no contact at all. You should be able to get some interest from your local paper, too, especially if there is a dearth of pop bands in your area.

Daniel Miller of Mute Records, who started out by releasing singles based at his flat, cites the example of one of his groups: 'Depêche Mode came from Basildon, where there are few bands. The local paper featured them every day. Local radio was good too, for a quick interview, but you have to have a bit of a following, be known locally. You could well get a local interview when national radio says no.'

Then you need to work out which radio and television programmes to approach. It's difficult enough to get everything right – the song, the production, the image, distribution, etc. – but the hardest thing, harder even than selling records, is to get your record heard.

Radio 1 evening shows such as *John Peel*, *Janice Long*, *Andy Kershaw* and *Anne Nightingale* are all worth approaching, as are the appropriate Capital programmes (whichever one suits your sort of music) and local radio. Throughout Britain daytime radio tends to concentrate on chart material and the big names, while evening slots cater for more minority tastes and the newer acts. Listen to the various shows carefully and choose discriminately.

Capital and other independent stations play more street music and are probably most up to date in terms of reflecting what is currently going on at grass roots. The BBC tends to play more established groups in the daytime, although some shows are starting to slip in records from brand-new bands.

Mike Hawkes, Janice Long's producer, says, 'It is best to send the record to the producer of the show. I listen to every single, and will give albums a cursory listen – there is no time to do more. Just send the record with a biography; photographs are not needed.'

Anne Nightingale will play new records that she thinks will sound good on her programme. Her criterion is: 'A record has got to jump out at me, grab my attention. I am looking for constant surprise, something which keeps my attention. I don't want to think I know what is going to happen next.'

To get your record played on daytime radio you will need to employ an independent plugger. Most record companies – large or small – agree that it is unlikely that an unplugged record will do anything on its own.

The reason for this is that there are so many records released each week that someone has to do the first sift for the poor overloaded producers: that is what a plugger does. The producer knows the pluggers and respects their views, so he will take what they say rather than spend time listening to an unknown, untried band.

If you go for television, buy the *TV Times* and *Radio Times* and make sure you send your record to the producer of whichever programme you decide your music is suitable for. Or you could ring up the programme beforehand, speak to the producer or production assistant and find out if they are interested in new bands at that time: if so, what name to approach. Most of these programmes run on a low budget, and since they have to pay union rates can get a known band for the same price as an unknown. But they do have periods when they are looking out for new music. It is worth checking.

Producing a video along with your single could be one way to get your record on to television, but it is not cheap (see Chapter 14).

SALES OUTSIDE BRITAIN

Britain still produces the highest-selling recording artists in the world, and although a few years ago the number of British artists in the American charts was larger than it is now, it is undeniable that Britain provides the major creative input of the business. Last year Britain earned £350 billion per annum in royalties from the success of British artists in the USA.

Small independent record companies rely on export to provide as much as 90 per cent of their income; 75 per cent is quite usual.

Foreign sales can be critical for a new band. For example, a small label in Britain might sell one out of four records in the home market, and three out of the four abroad, two of them to the USA. There are many more possibilities for independent labels in America, which has so many specialist outlets.

The main importers of UK products are, in order of importance, the USA, Japan and Europe (Germany, Holland and Italy, followed by Scandinavia – Sweden and Finland), then the rest, including Australia and New Zealand.

The three main export companies are based in London and you should approach them with your record as soon as it is pressed. As long as you have had some mention in the British music press and you are not completely unknown, you should get orders from foreign countries. Even a few hundred sales can help greatly with a desperate cashflow situation. If the major export companies won't take your record, try one of the smaller ones.

Export companies, which are listed in full in the *Music Week Directory*, will take white labels (records in white sleeves), put them on their new-release sheet and circulate this to their customers – by fax, weekly mail-outs, telephone, etc. These customers have access to the music press and if your record catches their attention they will put an order in – perhaps for just a dozen, perhaps for more. When the export company has collated the first few orders, it will buy that total amount off you (and probably about 25 for stock) at just under the UK dealer price. You must be prepared to sell at a realistic price, if the exporter is to be able to sell-on the product.

Having success abroad is very important, especially for small companies. Quite often it is far easier to sell records abroad than it is in the UK. Even the old super-group Ten Years After faces a big disparity in home and foreign sales, in favour of the latter: one of their recent CDs sold only 200 in the UK, while the same title sold about 6000 abroad.

So if your record starts to sell well in, say, Europe, you can use this information to drum up UK interest.

Check out which export company will suit your music best – whether it be dance, off-the-wall or more conservative material, for example. Each tends to specialize to a certain extent and a few telephone calls will soon establish which one you should approach.

CHAPTER 16

Lawyers and accountants

Lawyers and accountants are playing an increasingly important part in the record business. As has been the case in the USA for some years, they are becoming involved from the beginning of an act's career and several have got so embroiled by the business that they have ended up as managers, publishers and even running their own record labels.

LAWYERS

You should never, ever sign any document without taking legal advice: that cannot be too highly stressed. In fact, no record or publishing company, manager or agent of repute should *let* you sign anything without taking independent legal advice. After the last decade's run of expensive cases, most companies realize this has to be done if they are to protect themselves.

It is also important that you do not become too paranoid about getting the 'best' deal. Too much quibbling about the finer points could leave you with no deal at all.

Using an experienced music lawyer has more advantages than just the obvious one. If he has been involved in the business for some time, he will know just how far to push and how much to give – enough to keep the company *and* you happy. It can be done.

When choosing a lawyer, ask around, and see more than one if you are not happy with the first one you see. In any case, he might not like you. A lawyer should talk to you on the phone for five minutes, perhaps offering some general advice, without your incurring a bill. Try asking him anything about anyone; if he has the knowledge he should help you. Preliminary discussions should not cost you anything.

There are probably twenty music-business lawyers in London, but only half are worth talking to. You can find out which are the best ones by asking around and discovering which names continually crop up.

Don't be too frightened to ask a lot of questions. And don't worry if you think your questions sound silly: you've got to learn somehow, and everyone else started out knowing nothing at one time – although many soon forget that fact. Make sure you know what is going on; have someone to explain in detail what the negotiations are all about. Just because you are paying your lawyer good money, that doesn't mean you need know nothing about the contract. You must. Don't get fobbed off. If you don't understand, ask again until you are clear. You have to be absolutely sure about what you are signing, and understand the possible repercussions. Above all, remember that once signed your contract will be binding.

A lawyer is one person who will never ask you to sign a piece of paper. Either side can walk out on the other, although that happens very infrequently.

One of the top music lawyers offers a scenario of what usually happens with a fledgling band: 'A new group comes in to see me. They may say several record companies are interested, and perhaps they have been given a list of lawyers by the company or had a recommendation from a friend. I will ring up the record company, find out how serious it is, check out what sort of deal is being offered. A record company will be honest with a lawyer, maybe more so than with a group. I will see if what the record company is offering is reconcilable with what the group wants.

'They might ask, "Which record company should we go for – CBS or Rough Trade?" for example. I will tell them it all depends on what sort of music they produce and what they are aiming for. I will listen to them play. I have to place them on the musical spectrum for myself, to get a feel of what they are like.

'I see my job essentially as a translator of the needs and aspirations of the musician and reconciling them to those of the record company.

'Most bands are desperate to get into a studio and are

flattered by anyone who shows attention: that is where mistakes are made. Flattery gets in the way of their better judgement. A record contract can be the worst thing for them if it is not the right one.

'Ten years ago, I spent most of my time persuading groups not to sign. Now they are so cynical, full of legends passed down from band to band, I have to persuade them to sign.

'You have got to take a risk sometimes. It is a risk business and you must remember a record company is taking an enormous financial risk on you. It may be making a lot of money out of one successful group, but that has got to pay for all the failures. At the end of a year after signing a new band, a record company might have laid out as much as £300,000-£400,000. It would get better odds putting its money on an outsider in the 2.30!'

You can see why record companies take a long, long time before making up their minds to sign a band. They have a lot to lose.

Fees are the first thing to discuss with your lawyer. For the initial chat, it is unlikely that a lawyer will charge anything. After that he will usually charge fees in some kind of proportion to what you will be earning. And he will not send his bill until you have received your advance.

So don't be put off finding a lawyer early on because you are worried about being able to afford his fee. Until you receive some money from the advance you should not be sent a bill, and if the deal falls through the lawyer will wait until one is successfully negotiated – provided, of course, that you go back to the same solicitor.

If you are unhappy with the way your lawyer has handled your case, there is no necessity for you to return to him. But although he is unlikely to bill you – assuming you have discussed this right at the beginning – he is always entitled to do so.

The sort of legal costs you can expect to pay are about £1000 for a typical record deal; £600-£700 for a publishing one; and £300-£400 for a management deal. Don't forget talking to lawyers on the phone (once you have instructed them to handle your affairs) costs money. So rambling on when you could discuss something briefly is not a good idea. If you want to chat on in a friendly way, check first – you can do this in a casual way – that your chat isn't going on your bill.

Another lawyer describes how he operates: 'Normally groups find me through recommendation from other artists. I will listen to them play, at least once. You can't negotiate a deal effectively unless you know how they perform live and on record. I like to hear a demo as well. This way I know what their image is like and what they are like as individuals.

'It is important that an artist feels happy with his lawyer and *vice versa*, so I am quite happy to be sussed out first by them.

'Groups, or individuals, usually come to me before approaching a record company. They come when they've done a demo, and often ask which record companies they should approach. I'll listen to the cassette and see whether the material is commercial. I'll send tapes to record companies or, if the group is not ready, then possibly I'd pass them on to publishing companies.

'If they do not have a manager or are in a situation where the manager is not able – because of inexperience – to negotiate, I will do all the negotiating. If they have a manager with experience, I will suggest the line he should take, suggest he looks at various points in the contract – term, product, video, advance, royalties, etc. – and then leaves the details of the contract to me. A manager might well have had experience with two or three bands but not have negotiated contracts.

'I would recommend to new bands – if they have got something, but cannot interest a major record company – that they put out a single, preferably through an indi that doesn't want to tie you up, and just do a deal for that one single. At least, then, they can get plays, sales and, we hope, interest.'

The key is to establish contact with a lawyer as soon as possible. You don't need to have lengthy meetings, but an initial call or short meeting will give you some idea of what you are entering into, and you will know you have someone to turn to when necessary.

It is important to talk to as many people as possible, especially other bands which have progressed a bit further than you, but you will need someone with professional business and legal knowledge when you get out of your depth – which may happen more quickly than you think.

In the music business, one word in a contract can make a huge difference – and it is far better to sort out the problems before mistakes are made. Any artist should feel comfortable having creative meetings without his lawyer, but as soon as any discussion of the contract or other business matter is brought up he must declare that he has to talk to his lawyer. It won't deter the other party: in fact they should find it encouraging that you are taking things seriously.

A lawyer will provide basic accountancy advice, but if you are going to do a substantial deal he will give you a list of accountants to choose from.

ACCOUNTANTS

Accountants, along with lawyers, are another expense any band should be prepared to meet. A good accountant can save you far more money than you will ever spend on his bills. You will be amazed by the amount of tax an accountant can save you in the form of personal expenses offset against earnings. If you are aiming to hit the big-time, then an accountant should be brought in at the time you sign your first record deal.

Lawyers negotiate, accountants do not. Any decent lawyer will make sure that before a contract is signed you seek two sorts of financial advice – a tax structure and a financial structure. Experienced lawyers and managers know how far to stretch record companies, but are not so strong on the cashflow and tax side.

Nowadays accountants – like lawyers – are taking a far more personal interest in their clients. They are even seen at Midem – the yearly music-business festival at Cannes – mingling with record companies, publishing companies and the occasional group. They like to keep an ear to the ground and will always be on the lookout for new business.

There are quite a few accountancy firms in London specializing in the music business. An accountant from one of the top five explains: 'What normally happens is that we are approached by a group, or by their management, when they have got a demo tape. I will advise on which record company they should approach, if that is what they want, and put in a recommendation myself. If a record company shows some interest, I will give the group a list of lawyers, if they are looking for one.'

You might not think you need an accountant so early on. You are earning nothing, you know the advance you receive will be eaten up by recording costs and paying back debts already incurred – but you must always look to the future. The wording of the financial terms of your contract could make a difference of thousands of pounds later on in your career. One of the things you need to know, for example, is whether to sign as a partnership or as a limited company. At the moment it is advisable for groups to sign as a partnership, and when you become successful make yourselves a limited company. This situation could change if there are alterations in the tax laws.

Accountants will advise you on matters such as what to do with your advance. You do not have to pay tax on it for 18 months, so you could put it into a building society or deposit account meanwhile to earn interest, with a standing order for money to be paid out each month for you to live on. Your accountant will also compute your tax liability for the first year – which is important if you are not going to find yourselves suddenly with a huge tax demand. This money can then be tucked away earning interest until you need it. He can give you weekly or monthly pocket money, if that is what you want, so that you do not overspend – or at least help you budget through the year. Once old debts have been paid, equipment bought and other expenses dealt with you will usually have to budget fairly tightly to allow that first advance to keep you going. Sometimes managers will undertake to do this, but most prefer not to.

You should sort out at a very early stage how, as a group, you will share the profits on recording, merchandising, touring, public appearances, etc. It might seem an unnecessary detail to worry about at the time, but money from these sources could be forthcoming sooner rather than later, and if all this is in a contract it will make for an easier life later on. You might feel terribly democratic when you start out, agreeing to split everything equally between you, but if and when the money starts pouring in it is all too easy for greed to take over. Publishing is usually the most contentious area, as the writer is bound to want more.

When it is stated in the press that a group has split up because of 'musical differences', it almost always means money differences.

As soon as you start earning over a certain amount you will have to register yourself for VAT, and for that you will need an accountant. The present limit is £21,300, so it is not improbable that you could find yourself in that situation with your first advance.

How do you find an accountant? Ask friends in other bands, which are making money, which accountant they are with and whether they are happy with him. Or, if you have found a lawyer or a manager, ask him to recommend several to you. It is always worth double-checking a recommendation. But if you do not get on with the accountant when you first visit him, don't employ him. You should never use the same accountant as your manager or your record or publishing company: no one can be expected to do the best for both parties equally in the same transaction.

Your accountant, like your lawyer, should be sympathetic to and knowledgeable about the music business. It is vital that he knows what can be claimed, what can be offset against profits, and so on. An accountant who knows the industry can talk on a business level as well as a professional level. He will understand, for example, about tours making a loss, which can be offset against profits. He should also know about the international side of the business.

You may find it hard to think seriously about the financial aspects of your career when you start out. You are in a band because you love music, but the idea at the end of the day is to make money – not to lose it because of poor accounting, or, worse still, none. You should be able to work *with* your accountant, not against him. Knowing you have an accountant you can trust is also invaluable if you should suspect your record company, agent, manager, publisher or whomever of ripping you off.

Your accountant's fees should be discussed at your first meeting. When working out what advance you will need (or when your manager does so on your behalf) it is imperative that the fees you will have to pay for professional services are taken into account.

Since their charges relate to the amount of work they have to do – the time spent, the expertise needed – costs are not likely to be too high at the outset. And again, because of the business you are in, a music accountant will often delay putting in his bill until a deal is reached and your advance has been forthcoming. If your deal fails to come to fruition, it is unlikely you will have the money to be able to pay the accountant's bill, and most will consider this their loss. There is not a lot of point their trying to sue you for the money if you have none – like most young people at the start of their careers.

An accountant will be of the greatest assistance in the first 18 months, as that is the time when groups tend to have cashflow problems.

Here is one accountant's scenario of how the first 18 months of an album deal might go, moneywise, which puts in a realistic context the sums of money you may envisage earning. You should also bear in mind that advances are very often much lower than this fictional one – so don't blow a deal just because you have big ideas and think you are worth huge amounts of money.

On 1 January the band (of five people, let's say) receives an advance of £50,000. Its manager immediately takes his 20 per cent, £10,000 goes to old debts, £10,000 for new equipment: that leaves £20,000, which is not enough to keep five people going for a year. So you, the band, need to budget tightly.

It takes 3-4 months to record, 3-4 months before the album is complete, and in that time the record company might have put out one or two singles at a cost of £125,000 that you owe the company, in addition to the advance on royalties. That adds up to a minimum of £175,000, which you have to recoup. You certainly won't manage that on singles. There might also be video costs, together with travel fees, clothes, MU subs, etc. There will probably be delays in taking up options. So you may be forced into doing a publishing deal.

The accountant continues: 'I am often asked when to do that. I say it is better to do it after the record deal, even better after the first single, and perhaps after the second single or after an album. But if it flops, you are back to square one. It is a gamble against cashflow.'

Although it is tempting to hand over the responsibility of the paperwork to your accountant, you must make sure you know what your financial situation is at all times.

A manager worth his salt will be on the phone to your accountant continually. As one accountant admits plaintively, 'They are the bane of my life.'

CHAPTER 17

Contracts

Signing the right contract with the right company is one of the most important steps you will take in your career. You will be signing away a period of your life, and that could be a good part of your high-earning years.

Never sign a contract without thinking long and hard about it. It is all too easy to get caught up in the flattery syndrome. You may have been struggling for months, even years; suddenly, someone shows interest in you and offers you a contract. Of course, you jump at it. 'Somebody wants me,' you think: 'This is it!' – and before you know it your name is on the bottom of a contract.

First and foremost, however, you must consult a lawyer, and preferably one with knowledge of the music business. In the case of a recording or publishing contract, an accountant should be involved right from the beginning too.

There is no such thing, nowadays, as a standard contract. Some are only a few pages long, others can be as long as 60 pages! The points they cover include many variables, such as length of term (how long the contract is to run), options (on further songs or recordings), money (advance, royalties), how and when the money is distributed, etc., for both home (UK) and foreign sales.

When arguing points in a contract you need to be able to trade one item off against another. You can't expect everything you want to be agreed without your giving something back. Agreeing a contract is like a see-saw – it's all to do with give and take.

But be wary about changing too many things. An over-zealous lawyer, or one who is not experienced in the music business, might hassle at length about a tiny point that he considers important but which you are quite happy about; or he might cause so many problems for the company that it decides not to go any further. So find out what your lawyer is suggesting. It is better to be happy and have security rather than a few more pounds' advance or points on the royalty scale.

Remember that music is a business: record companies and publishers do not operate as a charity, they are there to make money – for themselves, as well as you. They won't give you a good deal unless you fight for it. They are not necessarily out to get you, just to protect themselves. That is why you do need to have someone (i.e. a manager or lawyer – a solicitor experienced in the legal aspects of the music business) who knows what he is talking about.

However, although you will have lawyers, accountants and probably managers to check the contracts you are signing, you must not think this gives you leave to remain ignorant of what you are signing. Find out what you are being contracted to do and how much it will tie you down.

After all the press coverage in the last decade of lengthy court cases involving star names and their record companies, publishers or managers, often with millions of pounds at stake, you would think that artists would make it their business to know what is going on. But there are still many cases of groups who have no idea what they have signed or what it entails.

A contract, once signed, is extremely difficult and costly to get out of, especially if it is not glaringly unfair to you and therefore worth court action. (For all those well-publicized cases, surprisingly few agreements end up in litigation.)

You are looking for a fair deal which is not excessively weighted in favour of either the record company, the publisher, manager, agent or whomever; but neither should you sign a deal heavily weighted to your advantage – although the chances of that happening are small – for there is bound to be a catch.

On the other hand, don't be too paranoid about getting ripped off. That way you'll never sign a deal, or if you *do* get offered one you'll be so suspicious and argue about so many points that the other party is likely to get fed up and decide not to bother.

There is never any hurry to sign. You are unlikely to lose

the deal simply because you need more time to think about it. If you are being pressurized into signing in a rush, don't do it. If a company is worried that somebody else will snatch you up, fine. Let the other company take you if it won't wait. But if you want to go with the first company, you can reassure the people concerned and there should be no problem.

RECORDING CONTRACTS

Most of the discussion that takes place on these will be about advances, royalties and length of term. When working out the advance you need, detail your costs for the first year and future years. The amount has to cover living expenses for all the members of the band, pay for the recording costs incurred on your first single/album, new equipment if you need it, and very possibly back debts as well. Work all this out carefully in advance and present your case clearly and concisely to the record company. If the record label really wants you, you should get something close, if not equivalent, to exactly what you ask for.

Royalties should not be below 8-10 per cent of the retail price (excluding VAT) of the single, album, cassette, CD, and could well be higher. A major record company may well give you a 12 per cent royalty on retail sales, although many now pay royalties on the wholesale price, in which case it should be about 15 per cent. Some contracts might specify the royalty rate in one clause: 'The company shall pay to the artist a royalty of 15 per cent for records sold in Great Britain and Northern Ireland and 7½ per cent for records sold to the rest of the world' and then clarify whether this is on retail or wholesale in a later clause. You might easily read the first paragraph and think you are getting a higher royalty than you actually are. Check also whether the producer's royalty will be taken out of it (this is usual in the case of a new band). A producer's royalty is about 2-3 per cent.

The minimum recording costs for a single would be £5000, and £25,000 for an album. Five years ago a single could be made in three days at a cost of a few thousand pounds, and an album for £5000. Much of this expense is due to the technology explosion, which not only increases costs but lengthens the time needed to record.

Some lawyers take the view that the royalty percentage is not as important as the royalty base (the unit on which the royalty is worked out – wholesale or retail price, usually) because record companies have so many ways of royalty accounting.

With foreign royalties, one problem area is reserves, another is that of withheld tax.

In those countries, particularly the USA, where record companies put their product into the shops on sale or return, they will try to cover themselves for the cost of returned stock by keeping a 'reserve' and paying artists only a percentage of the royalties earned. They use this device as a way of withholding payment – in fact, they have it down to a fine art – and it can take a long time before the full monies come through. It is therefore important to restrict this 'reserve' as far as possible. In some countries, of which Japan is a good example, record companies have to deduct tax, by law, from the records' retail price: this tax can be passed on to the artist and record company. It should either be shared pro rata between artist and record company; or, if the British record company can offset the tax itself, the artist should not be affected. Both these areas of the contract are highly complicated and need the attention of a professional, because the amount of royalties record companies hold back to deal with these problems can make quite a difference to when you receive your monies.

Royalties earned from foreign sales are normally paid at half the UK rate, but some small record companies have been known to add a clause on the following lines: 'The company has the right to license the record anywhere in the world and royalties from such sales would be computed at one-half the applicable royalty rate.' 'Anywhere in the world' can of course include the UK: therefore, by enacting this clause the company could in fact license your record to another UK company and pay you only half-royalties on your UK sales. To prevent this, the phrase 'anywhere in the world' should be deleted and 'anywhere outside the UK' substituted.

Royalties from abroad always take a long time to come through. Some of the major record companies account to the USA first, which exacerbates the time delay. Although there is little you can do about this – unless you are a well-established and very high-earning group – it could be argued that if the company is very slow in accounting it should pay a larger advance: it, after all, is using your money while you are being deprived of it.

Export is a huge market, especially as the percentage of all sales for newer bands can be as high as 75 per cent to begin with, so how you receive your money from abroad is important.

Another point to watch is the clause which specifies that the company will not pay royalties on a 12-inch single. This stems from the time when they were only a promotional gimmick, but some companies still try it on now. And some pay royalties for compact discs based on the vinyl price.

A lot of time will probably be spent arguing about reduced royalties for different types of sale, e.g. on record club sales you normally receive half-royalty, because such records are bought at a low price so that they can be offered to club members at a substantial discount; likewise, any record advertised on television is only liable for half-royalties: this may not seem important when you are a new group, but you could be famous within the year, when small details like this will count for a lot. You must always watch for clauses which will only begin to mean something when you are successful. You might laugh over an increased royalty which comes into effect at the point when sales over 100,000 have been made, but you'll be thankful when the record has sold its first million.

A point which is open to discussion and could be useful for trading-off is the packaging deduction – which one lawyer has described as 'the norm, but immoral'. This means that before your royalty is worked out a percentage is taken off the retail price of the record to pay for the packaging – sleeves, inserts, cassettes, etc. The more expensive the packaging – double gatefold, complicated inserts, for example – the higher the percentage. On a retail price, you are looking at a deduction ranging from 10 per cent for a single to 25 per cent for cassettes.

Promotional costs are sometimes paid for by the record company, sometimes by the artist, and clauses referring to these costs may be slipped in at the end of a clause relating to other matters; for example, '"recording costs" means all costs incurred by the company for and with respect to the production of master recordings of the artist's performances. Recording costs include, without limitation, the cost to the company of all instrumental musicians, vocalists, conductors, arrangers, orchestrators and copyists, all studio tape, editing, mixing, mastering, engineering, travel, rehearsal halls, costs of non-studio facilities and other similar costs in the production of the master recordings and all other promotional costs incurred by the company on behalf of the artist.'

This last cost could cover a multitude of expenses to be borne by the artist including promotional video recordings, reception and launch parties, etc. If these *are* to be included, specific sums should be mentioned.

It is important to retain as much artistic control as possible when you are dealing with a record company, although as a new artist you will not find this as easy to insist upon as it might be later on in your career. But you could try to retain your merchandising rights (sales from T-shirts, badges, posters, etc.) – a valuable source of income if you make it. Big-name bands can make more on merchandising than they do from record sales.

Merchandising is an excellent way of recouping money, and can be particularly lucrative in the USA. Although you need to have star status to make merchandising viable, it should be borne in mind right at the beginning of your career. You can always negotiate merchandising rights with your record company separately at a later date.

You can sign for a one-off single, or for as many as, say, eight albums, with options on the record company's side to get out of the contract after the first album. The first advance will relate to the first recording; any options taken up to record further singles or albums should elicit further advances and it is possible to renegotiate the contract at this point if the record company is keen to put out further albums. The majority of contracts nowadays are for about five or six album deals, or a period of eight years. That is a long time in a recording career, so you will appreciate how important it is to get the contract right.

Independent record labels tend to go for shorter contracts and much smaller advances, which often suits newer bands better. But however short the contract, never get bamboozled into not involving a lawyer.

For further information on recording contracts, consult *This Business of Music*, published by Billboard Publications (see page 178).

Having signed, try to keep in with your record company. It is the company personnel who have to sell your record, and if you have a choice of similar offers, how well you get on with the people could be a decisive factor.

MANAGEMENT CONTRACTS

A manager's contract should specify the manager's duties, otherwise you will be in danger of being tied to someone who does nothing. Once signed, it will be difficult for you to get out of the contract.

The most important thing to watch for in a management agreement is its length of duration and how the manager's percentage, usually 15-20 per cent of your gross earnings, is calculated; 25 per cent is too high, unless he undertakes to do other duties such as accounting or publishing, but if he does, make sure first that he is experienced enough to do this.

Most managers base their percentage on gross earnings (i.e. earnings before all deductions), which is extremely unfair – especially if you make a loss, which can easily be the case if you are touring. You will be out of pocket while your manager still takes his cut. If possible try to get his percentage taken from all, or just some elements of, your net earnings.

Managers will want a decent length of contract – usually three to five years. Otherwise, they argue, why should they do all the hard work in the first year, then watch you switch to someone else who will benefit from their efforts? Some managers will work with a new band for, say, a six-month period before signing contracts, just to see if they can work together. It would save a lot of unnecessary unpleasantness if more managers did this.

So watch for the clause which allows the manager to claim his commission on product which is released on a record label after your contract with him ends, but which he negotiated. That should not happen.

Management contracts are the most difficult to get out of. There should be a clause in the contract stating that if the manager has done nothing for you within a set period of time – the first year, for example – you can end the contract. By that time you could expect your manager to have procured an acceptable recording deal for you. There should be a clause on the lines of the following: 'The manager hereby undertakes to use all reasonable endeavours to obtain a recording deal with a reputable recording company within one year and if he shall fail to do so this agreement shall be terminated.'

Beware of the manager who promises deals in double-quick time. He may be able to get you one – how good it will be is debatable – but what then? He has had his cut from your advance and feels his work is done – which, of course, it isn't. Much of the hard work is still ahead. If you want to progress you need a manager who has the experience to take you further than just the first deal.

Production deals could be another problem. If your manager has his own record production company, he might well sign you to that and thereby put himself into an impossible situation. He will be torn, wanting the best for both you and the production company. It can lead to enormous trouble, and you shouldn't let that happen.

Beware also of the following clause in management contracts: 'Contracts arranged by the manager in respect of the artist's services may be with persons, firms or companies associated with the manager provided that they shall be upon terms which in the opinion of the manager are usual within the entertainment industry.' This means that the manager has *carte blanche* to sign any contract on your behalf without your knowledge or approval and gives you no right whatever to dispute any decision your manager may take on your behalf, nor would it be easy to hold him responsible for making a decision or signing a contract that is not in your interests.

PUBLISHING CONTRACTS

If you want some basic advice before going to a lawyer to discuss a publishing deal, PRS (the Performing Right Society) can be very helpful. Just ring up and say there is a contract in the offing and you would be grateful for some information on royalties, etc. Then, if you think it is worth pursuing, go to your lawyer.

If there is any rule to be followed on publishing contracts, avoid signing away your publishing for as long as you can. The more success you have, or the bigger buzz you can create, the better deal you will get. However, if you are having difficulty getting a recording deal, have written some good songs and desperately need the money, a publishing deal might help you get over a bad patch.

It is generally better to negotiate a publishing contract after you have made a recording deal, or, even better, after the release of the first single. But if that flops, you will be back to square one. Deciding which to go for first often boils down to a gamble against cashflow.

Some songwriters prefer to get a publishing deal first, to give them time and money to develop. Also, publishers are a little more approachable than record companies, and recording deals can take an age to tie up. If you are waiting for a recording deal and decide to go for a publishing deal in the meantime, you could regard your advance from that as seed money. You can then work around a bit to get a buzz going and thus hope to interest a record company.

If you do sign a publishing contract before making a recording deal, there should be something in the contract to assure you a better percentage and/or advance when a recording deal is clinched.

A publishing deal with an option after a year is best, though you will normally have to sign for three years. The option will always be on the publisher's side, but this is not a great disadvantage because if the deal is not working or you don't get on it will not want to keep you on its books any longer.

The main points to watch for are advance, royalties and length of term – not only the duration of the contract, but the number of years for which the publisher retains the copyright of your song. Publishers used to keep song rights for 50 years; now a much shorter period – ten or fifteen years – is more common.

As for a management deal there should be something in the contract referring to the work the publisher has to do, and provision for you to terminate the contract if he does not do it. A clause on the lines of the following should be included: 'The publisher hereby undertakes to use all reasonable endeavours to exploit the work and further undertakes to secure the release of a commercial recording through a reputable recording company, or the grant of a licence for the synchronization of the work with any television or film production or any motion picture; if the publisher should fail to secure at least one of the foregoing within two years then this agreement shall be terminated.' ('Synchronization' in this context means presentation – of the song or piece of music – that is linked with visual images.)

Publishers used to apportion income from publishing activities on a 50/50 basis, but now the more normal deal for a singer/songwriter is 60/40 or 70/30 (in each case to the artist's advantage).

A lot depends on precisely how the royalty is calculated: whether 'on receipts' or 'at source'. 'At source' means your British publisher will pay you your percentage on all the monies you earn, whether from Britain or abroad, before the foreign publishers take their cut. For new bands a 'receipts' deal is more usual, however. This means the publisher will pay you your royalty percentage on the money he receives from abroad after all the intermediary publishers have taken their cut. For example, if you are on a 60/40 deal and you make $100 in the USA the American branch might remit $75, of which you would receive 60 per cent (which is actually only 45 per cent of the original $100).

The clause referring to when the royalties are to be paid

should incorporate some sort of penalty in the event of the publisher not paying within a stipulated time period.

The following clause, for example, has no penalty: 'The royalties payable to the writer shall be paid within thirty days after receipt by the publisher of the monies on which the applicable payments are based and shall be accompanied by a statement showing how the same are made up.'

A better clause would be: 'The publisher shall pay to the writer all monies shown in half-yearly accounts within thirty days after the expiration of each half-yearly period. In the event that any payment is not made within the said period of thirty days, interest at the publisher's current bank's deposit rate shall accrue from the date that the payment became due until the actual date of payment and the publisher shall add the interest to the amount of the payment due.' (Accounting dates are often stated.)

Another undesirable clause is one which gives the publisher the right to alter a work without the author/composer's permission. The following clause, for example, is unacceptable as it stands: 'The publisher shall have the right to add, to take from, alter, adapt, edit, dramatize, transpose, arrange and change the words and/or music of the work in any manner that the publisher shall think fit and to provide and translate the lyric (if any) thereof into any and all languages.' If on the other hand it includes this proviso at the end: 'on the undertaking that the publisher has the prior written consent of the writer, such consent not to be unreasonably withheld', the clause is quite reasonable.

If you can avoid giving world rights to the publisher, do so. You can negotiate these separately when the time is ripe for you to sell them (that is, when you've had some success with a record), and probably at an advantageous royalty. However, most publishers will only take a new writer if he grants them all rights.

As an alternative to dealing with a publisher, you can set up your own publishing company. At its simplest, setting up a publishing company means that you, the writer, acquire a ready-made company (at a cost of about £250) then as soon as you have a number of songs recorded and ready for release you apply to become a member of PRS and MCPS as a publisher. Your lawyer can advise you further. As a publisher yourself you would deal direct with foreign publishing companies, which should reduce the delays on royalty payments enormously, and you would also receive mechanical royalties direct from the record company. Foreign publishing companies should take more interest in you as a fellow publisher rather than just as one of their many licensed acts. If you go abroad, the publisher should look after you (a friendly face is always welcome in a strange place), help with marketing, sales, and so on. Also, when you are touring foreign cities, the publishers will probably be there to help with promotion. Their direct link with you, the publishing company, means they might contact you with ideas – for using your work in commercials, etc. – which would not have happened otherwise.

Obviously self-publishing will not suit the majority of new groups: to do it successfully you need to have the contacts to set up the deals and to understand the international publishing scene. If, however, this is the case, and you have written a number of good songs which you feel are going to make an impression, then it is well worth considering because of the financial implications.

AGENTS

If you are still at a semi-professional stage you certainly do not need to sign with any agency as you will be able to secure most of the gigs yourselves.

Most of the bigger agencies will demand contracts, but you can try putting off signing a long-term agreement for as long as possible, just signing one for each gig, or batch of gigs, that they arrange for you. You need to be reassured that your agent will offer you something in return for signing with him – in other words, have him prove he can get you work first, otherwise you could find yourself tied to one who does nothing for you and could thereby deprive you of work and income. Try not to sign for longer than three years; some of the leading agents are now asking for (and occasionally obtaining) contracts for as long as five years.

The agreement you will have to sign for each gig the agency sets up for you will include details such as date, venue, time, length of performance, the fee and when it will be paid. An agent's commission is usually 10 per cent and should certainly not be more than 15 per cent of the fee paid. Be on the lookout for a clause referring to other performances you may wish to do within a specified radius of the venue during a period before and after your gig: a 15-mile exclusion in rural areas might be quite reasonable, but in London it would be absurd. Such a clause might read: 'The artist shall not without the written consent of the management perform at any other public place of entertainment within a radius of 15 miles of the venue during a period of eight weeks prior to and eight weeks following this engagement.'

VENUE AGREEMENTS

If you have no agent and are securing gigs yourself you may be asked to sign agreements. These should specify when and where you will be playing, for how long, for how much, and when the money will be paid. The form of words should be quite straightforward and will usually be in the form of a letter.

If you are doubtful whether a pub, for example, will honour arrangements made verbally, it is a good idea to write a letter to the above effect and ask the publican or booker to sign a copy of it before the gig. This should prevent arguments later. Strictly speaking, if either side has to cancel 14 days' notice should be given. On the whole, leeway will be given by the booker if there is a very good reason for the band's cancelling, such as illness. If you have an agent and your venue/booker cancels at the last minute, the agent will usually sue. It is generally more difficult for the venue to cancel than for the band to do so.

CHAPTER 18

Allied activities

So far the assumption has been that you are reading this book because you want to become a rock star. But there are of course many other areas of the music business, allied to performing, in which musicians, songwriters and composers can operate.

SONGWRITING

Any band hoping to make it needs good songs. These may be written by a member, or members, of the band – which is what usually happens nowadays. The singer/songwriter is now the norm rather than the exception.

If none of you feels you are capable of producing that hit song yourselves, you will have to look for one from another writer. If you are with a record company, it will look for you, using publishing contacts. Otherwise, your manager might suggest someone he knows who he thinks writes songs suited to your sort of style. If you do not have a record company or a manager who can help, you will have to try friends, or friends of friends, who might be able to come up with a song for you.

If you see yourself as a songwriter, you will need to build up a collection of songs, work on them and prune or polish them as necessary. Be highly critical about them yourself, and ask respected friends to listen and comment – preferably constructively. It is difficult to judge your own work objectively, but the best songwriters are the ones who are able to do that.

As Tony Macaulay has observed: 'The most important thing is not to fall in love with your own songs.' You must be able to adapt a song if someone wants you to. The song is not the be-all and end-all. You are just writing words and music: neither is sacrosanct.

One of the best ways to improve your writing is to collaborate with another writer. Think of all the successful writing partnerships there have been: Lennon/McCartney, Benny Andersson/Bjorn Ulvaeus, Nile Rodgers/Bernard Edwards, Dominic Bugatti/Frank Musker, Andrew Lloyd Webber/Tim Rice, Mike Chapman/Nicky Chinn, Don Black/Geoff Stevens, to name just a few.

When you are starting out, try writing with as many different people as possible to find a partnership that works. In this way you can criticize and help each other, bounce ideas off each other and generally improve what you do.

By using contacts and trying to meet as many people as possible you will widen your chances of being able to write with others. Finding the right partnership is not easy. Just writing with a known writer, for example, does not necessarily guarantee success, although it often helps.

Scarlet, a singer/songwriter who tried writing with an assortment of people, including one of the top writers, describes how she eventually found her successful partnership with Red and they formed the group Red Scarlet: 'I decided a few years ago the best thing was to write with as many people as possible. I was still managed by Alan Seifert but was not happy, so I asked him to find me people to write with. He gave me a list, and I rang the first name on it – Dominic Bugatti. I called him up and said, "Can I meet you and play you some of my songs?" He was stunned. We chatted a bit and seemed to get on, and he said he would call back. I never thought he would.

'A week later I got a call from him, saying he had a spare half-hour and could I come over? It just worked, we liked each other, and I wrote with him for seven to eight months. By this time in my career I had learnt quite a lot about being ripped off, so I asked Dominic for 50 per cent of every song we wrote, right from the beginning. Amazingly, he drew up a contract, and even made a little video to help me show people what I looked and sounded like. At that time I was living by working for the Gas Board and doing session work.

'The problem was that every finished product was good,

but nothing special, and all the songs were in a different style. Publishers all said we were OK as a writing team, but I wanted to be recognized as an artist/writer. I wanted to perform my songs, not hear somebody else doing it.

'Then I met up with Red and we started writing together. Everyone who listened to our tapes said, "This is it." I had found the right combination.'

Writing with other people will give you confidence, especially if he or she is relatively successful. If you get a cover (i.e. somebody records your song), it will probably be because of the known writer – but it will still be good for your ego. Also, the other writer will probably have a publishing deal already and therefore be able to help you get one, either with him or on your own. As in all other areas, a recommendation from somebody well-known will get you miles further than a cold approach.

Ideally you should have a manager to tout your songs around. It is very difficult to ask for money for yourself – especially as a songwriter, when the song you have created is something which has come from your soul. How can you go in and act the hard businessman about your 'baby'? A manager can, however.

Other necessary qualities are persistence and stubbornness. As one writer says: 'I had a really tough time to start with. After the first two years of writing, any normal person would have given up. I refused to.'

After writing your songs, you need to persuade a publisher to take on your work. For this you will need tapes, which must represent the very best of your work and be well recorded; limit the number of songs on your tape to a maximum of three (most publishers say that if there are more than that they will not listen to the tape – or, if they do, and the best song is the last one, they will have lost concentration).

One writer comments: 'You need a sympathetic publisher who will loan you money while you are waiting for it to come in from other sources. If you are working and see some success in the future, don't give up your job until you really have to, and never spend too much time on a song. Being versatile is not that important. Writing a song which can be covered *is*.'

If you are lucky the publisher will pay you a small advance, and further money if the publisher accepts more songs or if you have some success as a performer. You might even get a small weekly retainer if the publisher really thinks you have got something. As a new writer, you must have a publisher who will work your songs. He has to know at what time to send which singer the right song. For example, a writer co-wrote a song with a friend for which they had Helen Terry in mind. They sent it to Virgin Records but heard nothing. A few months later the writer met the A & R person at Virgin, and while chatting discovered he was looking for songs for Helen. She gave him the song she had sent in earlier and Terry recorded it.

If you do not have a good voice, then you will have to find someone to sing your songs. Try friends who will do it for nothing, in the hope that if the song gets somewhere you will pay them something. Watch and listen to other bands, and if you like a particular voice, approach the singer, who will probably be happy to sing your material for you. The publisher who eventually takes your songs could also be interested in the singer – or band – who performed it.

If you can't pay the singer you should at least help him as much as possible by letting him have a copy of the song first and giving him the key, so he can practise and therefore be able to record it quickly. If the backing track is already recorded it should only take an hour to lay down the vocals. Allow another hour to do the final mix.

'You must get the best possible singer available,' stresses one writer. 'I have spent a lot of money getting singers to sing my songs, but it has been worth every penny for them to sound right.'

The union rate for singers is at present £55 for three hours' work but they often charge much more – up to £200. You should always be able to find someone who can sing well in your area. Established singers will often do demos with people starting out, too, as this is one way for them to find new songs.

It is worth spending a lot of time making demos. You do not have to have loads of expensive equipment – just loads of time. Some very experienced writers, such as Terry

Britten, for example, make their demos to the standard of a master.

Ideally your demo tapes should be perfected to the same degree, until the production sounds like a record. Make sure the mix is right – each sound balancing well and the singer's voice clearly audible. There should be no hiss and no sloppy notes. The final tape should be exactly as you want it to sound: it is no good saying, 'Well, if the piano was tighter, or the guitar louder, it would sound better.' The sound must be 100 per cent right when the publisher hears it, which is why you need to invest so much time in the exercise. Most successful songwriters, aware of the importance of producing first-class demos (without having to keep one eye on the studio clock), now have their own 8- or 16-track studios at home.

Once your tapes are made, you can of course send them to other writers, producers or managers, besides music publishers.

One established writer/producer comments: 'The majority of publishers are always interested in new writers, and can send your songs to other songwriters. I will always listen and if they are any good will try to help – recommend where to go.'

Most publishers prefer singer/songwriters, but there are still a few writers, not many, who make a good living just writing songs.

It is notoriously difficult to get people to record your songs commercially: they always want to sing their own material. But even singers such as Paul McCartney and Elton John have recorded other people's songs. So it is always worth persisting.

If you should get one, or several, of your songs recorded, remember that the royalties could continue to come in for years afterwards. Cat Stevens, for instance, who has been out of the business now for over ten years, still receives royalty cheques for substantial sums. But it can take two years for the first royalties to appear, especially from abroad.

Unless you are one in a million, you will never get a fat cheque for royalties: they will trickle in gradually, so look at royalties as your pension plan.

Signing a publishing deal with a large publisher is not necessarily better than signing with a small company, which might be expected to take a more personal interest in you. One writer who signed with Chappell recalls: 'My deal came up for renewal and I had an option to leave. I was very disappointed in the company, as it had done no work for me for two years. Then I signed with Perfect Songs for two years, with an option on the third. I thought that signing with a publisher attached to a record company should mean covers by their artists of my songs. But it didn't work, as so many artists want to use their own stuff.'

Finding a publisher who is really enthusiastic about your songs and keen to work them is obviously of prime importance. You must be prepared to try several before you find one who likes you, as well as one with whom you are happy.

Billy Livsey, a successful American writer and producer who has been working in Britain since 1980, started by working for the publishers E.H. Morris. He listened to twenty demos a day, working out what each song was all about: 'I would recommend it. It is good experience. All the time I was writing my own songs, submitting them to other publishers and getting rejection slips. Rejections can be good for you: you either get angry or think, "I'm going to show you!" They make you work harder.'

Even a successful writer will get lots of rejections, so you must learn early on to accept them philosophically.

Livsey played in an assortment of bands and met other writers that way: 'Not only did I make lots of contacts, but I could learn how songs are constructed, etc. It was very worthwhile. There is no replacement for experience. But a lot of the time is just spent waiting for the phone to ring.'

As a songwriter you will also need a lawyer and accountant from early on in your career. Planning for the future is essential, even when you are not earning money. Should you get your song on that hit single or album, you need to be set up so that you can make the most of the money.

If you want to be a songwriter and you are proficient in one or more instruments (to at least Grade 6 standard), it could be an idea to think about going to a music college. You would then be able to learn about many different areas of music, including orchestration and improvisation, as well as improving your abilities as a performer. Your musical horizons will also be vastly extended. All in all, the experience can only strengthen your chances of getting work later.

Apart from the Royal Academy of Music, Royal College of Music, Trinity College of Music and Guildhall, all in London, which require extremely high entrance standards, there are several polytechnics and universities – Manchester and Surrey, for example – which now run general music courses. Leicester University was one of the first colleges to run a course incorporating pop music, Perth College the first to run a rock music course.

As for any further education, you need to be competent in your subject: the Guildhall, for example, needs a minimum of Grade 5 instrumental proficiency and 5 O-levels (which need not be in music). However, if you are particularly competent in one instrument, leeway might be allowed in other qualifications. You could also obtain a Performance Diploma by working with a private teacher. Leicester requires a minimum of two A-levels including music and Grade 6 in one instrument; for Surrey you need three A's, in maths, music and physics.

Your local education authority will provide information on colleges that run music courses.

You might want to devote your life to songwriting, but if you can sing or do session work you will at least be able to earn a crust during all those years when you are building up your repertoire.

SESSION WORK

Doing session work is one of the best ways of making contacts, but you need to be an accomplished musician (and an MU member) as well as a good hustler in order to break into this somewhat cliquey field. Many established groups use session musicians for recording *and* live gigs: they find it less of a hassle than having, say, two more full-time members of a band.

New bands sometimes use good professional session players too. If they are making a demo, for example, shortage of both money and time means it can be worth their while to pay for a session musician who works fast rather than wasting pounds with an inexperienced member of the band who will take hours to get things exactly right.

In addition to the fixers (see page 162), there is one agency, at the time of writing, which puts together session musicians and bands, for showcases, studio work, filling in for a tour if someone falls ill, and so on; similarly, someone looking for session work might find it worthwhile to contact Nu-Line Promotions (see page 179).

Minimum fees, covering overtime, overdubbing, etc., are determined by the Musicians' Union and vary depending on whether you are recording an album, playing for TV or radio, doing a live gig or making a jingle.

An album session rate, for example, is currently £55.30 for three hours. An overdub is 125 per cent of that basic rate, a second overdub 150 per cent. The MU will quote you its rates over the phone. For doubling – for instance, playing both acoustic and electric guitar – there is a small extra fee. There is no longer a different rate for demos and masters.

Alternatively you can come to some agreement for an all-day fee. But it is advisable – for your own sake and that of other musicians – not to drop below the basic rate. This creates problems for other people as well as for yourself. You should in fact try to charge slightly more than the basic, though you will not be able to do this if you are just starting out.

The main qualities for a session musician are adaptability, amenability and professionalism. You are being paid for playing as required, not as you might feel you should.

Be on time for the session, and if you are working with a new musical director or producer turn up at the studio at least half an hour early. That way you can make friends with the engineer and perhaps make him an ally. And when the producer arrives, usually a little early too, ask to see the chord charts or score of the arrangement so you can check out anything that may be particularly difficult, while there is still peace and quiet. Once all the other musicians start arriving, there will be too much happening to allow you to concentrate.

Always be polite, and remember to thank the person you have been working for. Diplomacy is vital.

If working for the BBC, ITV or main radio stations, you just provide your name and address and you will automatically be paid the MU agreed fee.

Any other employer will have to be invoiced, so it is important to find out for whom you are doing the session. You may be booked by another musician, but he will not necessarily be the person who is paying you.

One successful session musician reveals that he got started through word of mouth but found he couldn't earn a living by relying on that method. It was only when he sent a tape to a fixer (booking agent) that he started making money: 'About a year after sending the tape I had a reply. Through that fixer I met musical directors, other artists, producers, other fixers, etc., who then called me direct.'

Songwriters sometimes start working with various bands as session players. One who is now also a performer and producer comments: 'There is a very well-established grapevine, and session-playing is one way to meet people, take telephone numbers and get yourself known. It is terribly difficult to start with. You just have to get out, talk to as many people as possible and make contacts. There is a lot of waiting around.

'I began to get involved doing arrangements for bands, which I could do because of my music college training. I then thought, "Why not try writing?" It was something to do in my spare time. Writing for me comes from a professional rather than a spiritual urge.'

The way to find a fixer or contractor is to ask around, or ring up your local MU office, which can recommend reputable ones, and send off your tape. It should be a mixed bag, including 30-second snippets of you playing different types of music: jazz, classical, funk, etc. The better presented your package, the better your chances of marketing your talent.

Fixers go very much on recommendation, however. You may have taken days to put down the music on a tape, but this does not guarantee you can work fast or play well at sight. Incidentally, fixers do not charge the musicians. They charge between 10 and 12½ per cent of the overall cost to their client.

Although it is a great advantage to be able to 'read', i.e. play at sight, from either a score or a chart, it is not essential as chord charts rather than a proper score are often used nowadays. But do check whether sightreading ability is required before you accept a booking. Usually the scores will be quite simple, although you must be prepared for about 10 per cent difficult work. Try to keep up with all the latest 'toys' and effects, too: if you hear a very unusual guitar sound, for example, used on a hit, do your homework and make sure you can reproduce it, or fluff something similar. That's one way of impressing producers.

Also, you must be able to play different versions of your selected instrument – both acoustic and electric guitar, for example, and both fretless and fretted bass; you should be able to program a keyboard as well as play it, and use both a drum kit and a drum machine.

Don't drink too much on a session. If there's a lunch break, eat as well. The producer may well be keeping the tough bit till the afternoon, thinking that by then you will have gained confidence and loosened up a bit. It's no good not being able to get your brain and fingers together because you have had a boozy lunch.

A top session player recalls: 'One keyboard player I know always used to turn up to sessions pissed out of his mind. Or if he wasn't when he started, he certainly was by the end. I asked him one day how he managed to play like that. He told me, "I just practise when I'm pissed!" But not many musicians can work like that.'

LIBRARY MUSIC

Library music is an area where you can earn some extra income, but you do need to be an experienced writer of instrumental music. It may not be creatively satisfying, but it should earn you a little pocket money. However, writing library music is nearly as hard to get into as songwriting.

Library music is music written specifically for inclusion in audio or audio-visual productions and is used when a company cannot afford to commission an original score for dramas, documentaries, training films or jingles, for example.

There are about thirty library-music publishers in Britain who produce albums of background mood music: KPM and Bruton Music, for example, are two of the largest, and MCPS has a list of those publishers which are members. These companies keep albums covering a multitude of different types of music – fanfares, 'baroque', romantic, and so on. Clients (jingle company or audio-visual company, for example) can therefore go directly to the specific type of music they need.

Library music companies all work on slightly different lines. However, a member of one of the biggest explains that his firm operates on the following basis: 'We do not pay any composition fee, but if your composition is used you will then receive 50 per cent of the royalties due. We, as the publisher, receive the other 50 per cent.'

To get your work into the catalogues of the various library music companies you need to send them cassettes or tapes of music you have composed. They will listen to what you can do and if they like your work commission you to write something on a specific line.

The standard of recording on your tape is not as important as the music itself, as the company – if it likes your material – will take on the expense of recording, marketing, etc. That is why you only receive 50 per cent of any monies due. This is paid through MCPS, so you have to be a member of that organization (see page 178).

Although you can make a living from it, writing library music will never make you rich. What it will give you is invaluable writing experience.

JINGLES

To write jingles you need to be able to write a catchy tune that lasts from 10 seconds to a minute. That's not very long, if you have been used to writing songs. To do well at it, you should be able to arrange music.

Jingles are normally commissioned by advertising agencies or film production companies. It is also possible for writers to work direct for local commercial radio stations, which produce a certain proportion of their advertisements in-house. ILR is in fact often a good way to start. Jingle-writing is something you usually get into through contacts. If you don't have the contacts you will have to work through a list of jingle companies, send in tapes of your work, ring and hustle for attention. Most companies use writers they know or are recommended to, so a cold approach is unlikely to get you very far.

As a musician, if you are doing a jingle session, you will be paid a 'three-year buy-out' (i.e. if the jingle is used after the three-year period ends, you should receive another payment; jingle musicians do not receive repeat fees as actors and singers do). The rates are governed by the MU, and you should be paid more for a master than a demo.

AUDIO-VISUAL WORK

Audio-visual work (film scores, television theme music, music for conferences, etc.) is another avenue you could follow as a writer, and it could, of course, be combined with a career in rock.

It is an area in which writing experience is essential, and, yet again, making the right contacts and being in the right place at the right time are just as important as musical skills.

One songwriter who does audio-visual work describes how he got started: 'I was writing songs and trying to get myself a recording contract when a good friend of mine asked me to write the theme to a television series. The original score had not come up to scratch. I still had to audition – I sent in a demo of my work which I thought appropriate. And I got the job, but I had not intended to go into that side of the business.'

If you intend to approach the business from cold you need a good tape of your current music to send around to the production companies. From then on, be prepared to hassle. If you find this difficult, maybe a manager or agent could help – but it's like the chicken and the egg: do you get the track record or the manager first?

The weekly magazine *Screen International* is one trade publication which would be worth reading, and Maclaren, the publishers of the monthly magazine *Audio/Visual*, also put out a comprehensive directory listing production companies, etc. which commission music (see page 178).

Even if you are lucky enough to get a break, you will find that there is usually very little money in audio-visual work until you are well established. However, you will get repeat fees for any work that is played more than once, and for television or radio themes, for example, the sums could mount up substantially.

CHAPTER 19

Music organizations

There are over forty organizations, at the time of writing, connected with the popular music industry in Great Britain, but the following are the ones you are most likely to come across or need to contact. Addresses and telephone numbers can be found at the end of this section.

BASCA

The British Academy of Songwriters, Composers and Authors was founded in 1947. Its primary aim is to provide advice and guidance to writers.

A simple standard publishing contract has been devised by BASCA for its members' reference, and it also has a solicitor whom member-writers can contact, initial consultations being free.

BASCA is funded by members' subscriptions and PRS. There are two levels of subscriptions: associate membership (£11.50 per annum) and full membership (£12 per annum plus 2 per cent of the member's PRS earnings up to a maximum of £35). The subscriptions for full membership are collected yearly through PRS. Membership is open to anyone who writes music or lyrics.

BASCA holds regular 'surgeries' attended by established songwriters who will review tapes, offer advice and answer questions; it also issues a quarterly magazine to its members and presents the Ivor Novello Awards.

BPI

The British Phonographic Industry, a limited company, was formally inaugurated in 1973, when there was a sudden upsurge of record companies which found they needed their interests represented as a whole. It now represents over 120 record companies in the UK.

One of the most important duties of the BPI is to protect its members against piracy and counterfeiting. In phonographic terms, piracy means putting out unlicensed copies of a record, usually in countries where there are weak or non-existent copyright laws; counterfeiting means copying a record exactly, right down to the label and logo, and selling off the whole package as the original. In neither case would any form of contract exist with the original record company, nor would any money be paid. The practice makes it difficult for a legitimate industry to operate. In Britain there is very little piracy: it is mainly confined to the cassette market, where it represents about 1-3 per cent of product. The racket is most virulent in the Middle East and Far East; in Singapore, where thousands of Western commercial recordings are re-recorded on to blank cassettes on ordinary domestic tape-recorders every year for retail sale, piracy accounts for as much as 90 per cent of the market.

Counterfeiting has changed in Britain from small- to big-time over recent years. Terri Anderson, previously press officer for the BPI, explains: 'Originally counterfeiting used to be a little cottage industry carried out by people on the fringe of the business; they were easy to find and deal with. Since 1980 counterfeiting has become part of established criminal activity. There are fewer people involved, but they operate on a bigger scale and they are usually tied up with some other criminal activity such as forged currency.

'For years we could only pursue the perpetrators through civil law. But in 1983 an Act was passed which acknowledged a certain degree of criminal intent. Conspiracy is the usual charge, now resulting in a prison sentence.

'Home taping is much more of a problem in Britain than either piracy or counterfeiting.'

BPI realizes it cannot hope to stamp out home taping, especially with more and more reasonably priced high-tech equipment being produced (DAT – digital audio tape – is the most recent threat). However, there are now moves to encourage software manufacturers to incorporate a spoiler system in pre-recorded tapes to prevent copying.

BPI and the other associations representing both writers and artists have been endeavouring since the late 'seventies to establish a small levy on blank tapes to recompense the industry for some of the millions of pounds it loses yearly through home taping. The industry is looking for a 10 per cent levy, i.e. 10 per cent of the retail price of a blank tape. Whether it will be the importer, the manufacturers or the consumers who eventually pay for this remains to be seen. However, it does seem fair that writers of music and/or lyrics should be compensated to some degree for the huge loss of revenue for which the home taping brigade is responsible.

The BPI is also concerned with the continual battle over hyping (manipulating the charts illegally), altering the rules to keep up with the wiles of the companies, reprimanding and fining them – in extreme cases – if they step over the mark significantly. Although both the BPI and most record companies deny that hyping exists nowadays to any great extent, it certainly does go on, especially at the lower end of the charts.

One record company director views hype as a valid form of marketing: 'I consider it to be just another business gamble. A single is like an advertisement for the album, so you pay for it to achieve the best advantage. If a single is hyped, the record company takes more interest in the group, because it is costing them more.

'Merit is what counts in the end, but you cannot sell just on that. You have to help things along. The top twenty should be interference-free, but the lower charts oil our industry. Hyping provides a service to labels, because they can load presses according to volume.

'From 20 to 30, any interference is a reflection of teenage mood rather than broader public sales; 50-75 needs to be hyped to let media know what records have been selected for other people to choose. With 110 singles released every week, someone has to choose which records might have a chance.'

Although not many people would openly agree with hyping, it is the buying-in at the top end of the charts – a very expensive operation – that most are against, and this has certainly been curtailed to a large extent.

The BPI's stated objective is 'to make sure that hyping doesn't work, rather than to stop it: to make it ineffectual. Constant attempts are still being made, but they are relatively ineffective. It is not only record companies, but friends of groups, grannies, etc. buying large quantities of one record.

'No one would claim that the chart is 100 per cent accurate every week, but we would say it is as accurate as is humanly possible.'

MCPS

The Mechanical Copyright Protection Society was formed in 1924 when two companies, the Copyright Protection Society and the Mechanical Copyright Licences Co Ltd, were merged. Since 1976 it has been wholly owned by the MPA (see separate entry). It currently employs a staff of about 180 and represents 6000 composer members and 4500 publisher members based both in the UK and abroad. It also represents many thousands of foreign composers and publishers through reciprocal agreements with overseas societies.

Mechanical copyright is the right to record and MCPS collects royalties which it distributes, after commission has been deducted, to its members every time a musical work is recorded, whether on to record, cassette, video or CD or for a broadcast or any public performance. It employs a field force which is in contact with local radio stations, television companies, production companies, video companies, etc.

An MCPS executive explains: 'We only have five people going round Britain, but we do have agreements with pressing plants which inform us monthly which companies they have pressed for, not artists or tracks. We also have agreements with users of library music, etc. So we get a pretty good feedback. Also we have people ringing in all the time reporting on recordings being made. One man rings once a week. So there's quite a grapevine to rely on.'

MCPS has a blanket agreement with the BBC and Independent Television Companies Association by which they (the BBC and ITCA) pay an annual royalty sum to MCPS in return for relatively unrestricted recording of its members' works. Record companies are issued with licences, the major record companies paying a licence fee dependent on the number of records sold and the smaller companies paying according to the number of records pressed. Revenue is also collected from background-music companies, video companies, even churches where a video with music might be made of a wedding or a bar-mitzvah. The revenue collected for 1986 was in the region of £15,000,000. At the time of writing it is possible for publishers to collect direct from eight of the major record companies.

MCPS distributes royalties to either the publisher or the writer of a work, not both, once a month. If you just need a collection agency for your royalties then you need to be a member of MCPS and PRS. One advantage of being a member yourself is that you will receive your money more quickly. If it goes through your publisher you will have to wait three or six months for his accounting dates, as stated in your contract. If you need your works promoting at home and abroad, then you need the help of a publisher.

As a writer you need to have three or four works recorded which are earning royalties before MCPS will accept you as a member. Membership is free. It is up to you to keep MCPS aware of all works of music you create and details of any publishing arrangements, using the standard work notification card sets which you obtain from PRS and sending one copy of each to MCPS.

The royalties MCPS collects in Britain are a statutory 6¼ per cent on the price of each record sold, excluding VAT, and are divided between the owners of all the copyright tracks. So if you are only responsible for the A side of a single, you will receive half that amount; if yours is one track on a twelve-track album, you will get one-twelfth of that amount. If there is a large number of very short tracks on one album, a minimum royalty of 0.313p is payable, which could add up to more than 6¼ per cent. Outside the UK the royalty rates differ: for example, the current European average is 8 per cent, while in America it is 5 cents per track or 0.9 of a cent per minute, whichever is the greater.

MCPS has agreements with all foreign mechanical-royalty collection agencies which operate in countries where copyright is recognized. The foreign agencies pass on any royalties due to British artists while MCPS does the same for foreign artists.

MPA

The Music Publishers' Association was started in 1881 and it bought MCPS in 1971. It is a trade association set up to promote and protect music publishers, but as Peter Dadswell, MPA's company secretary, explains, 'It keeps a close watch on the songwriter. It is often thought to be just on the side of the publisher, but I feel a duty to be aligned to songwriters as well.'

Any music copyright owner can be a member of the association. Individuals can go to the office or ring up for advice, but will normally be recommended to find a publisher or become a member if they intend to publish their own work. If you are looking for a publisher the MPA has a list of 200 members which it will supply on request, together with other information relevant to music publishers. It will also give advice on how to set up your own publishing company, although this is not something it recommends to inexperienced songwriters.

MUSICIANS' UNION

Set up in 1921, the Musicians' Union has three functions: to represent musicians, to negotiate on their behalf and improve their lot, and to help individual members. It will accept any musician who is playing for money and prepared to pay his yearly subscription rate.

As a member you are guaranteed certain agreed rates for specified types of work, whether in radio or television, gigs (although these are often flouted at the smaller venues), rehearsals, dubbing, miming, doubling or whatever. You can register musical equipment up to the value of £400 for insurance at no extra cost and claim sickness or accident benefit if you have been a member for at least six months.

Subs are graded according to yearly earnings from music. For 1986 there were four scales, ranging from £30.26 a year for musicians earning up to £60 a week (from music) to £93.70 a year for those earning £210 or more per week.

The Union provides a free advice service to members on subjects such as rates of pay and insurance and has a full-time legal department to advise on contracts, although it cannot negotiate for you.

If you wish to perform on television or radio you will generally find it necessary to be a member of the union before you are allowed to appear, though it is possible that you will not be asked. A video to be broadcast on television must first be seen and registered by the Union and the correct forms signed before it may be used. The MU has been heavily involved with establishing performance fees for musicians who play on videos.

There are 121 branches of the MU in Britain. When you join you will become a member of the relevant branch, and although in theory you should be able to ring any branch for advice or guidance, in practice this is not always the case. Some branches are more helpful than others, but if you do have any problems you should ring the national office in London.

PPL AND VPL

PPL (Phonographic Performance Ltd) and VPL (Video Performance Ltd), which was only formed in 1984, provide another source of royalties for the singer/musician.

Although these two companies primarily represent record companies, which have a copyright interest in the records they make and therefore receive the lion's share of the net distributable income, PPL also makes a small ex-gratia payment (20 per cent of that income) to artists. It is up to the record companies to inform PPL about the artists on their labels, but an artist who is not receiving any payment can always ring PPL to check whether his name is on its computer. The amount an artist might receive could vary from £5 to thousands of pounds, depending on how many times the artist's record is broadcast and how much money is in the pool to be distributed.

PPL was formed in 1934, its first members being the three major record companies of the day – Decca, EMI and

Brunswick, the latter long since defunct. It is concerned only with original recordings (i.e. the sound recording which the artist concerned played on, whether record, tape or CD) and royalties earned from their being broadcast or used in public performance. It now has 600 record company members and will only represent those that are registered in Britain or the EEC.

A foreign artist signed with a British company will therefore receive royalties, but a successful group whose record is widely played in Britain but which is signed with an American company, for example, will not.

PPL is a much smaller operation than PRS, having only 50 staff, and it works closely with the BPI (see separate entry), striving for better rates and agreements relating to new ventures such as cable and satellite television stations, protecting its members' rights and funding anti-piracy campaigns.

PPL licenses broadcasting stations, which (in contrast to the procedure for PRS) have to notify PPL of every record played – whether they are the BBC or a tiny local radio station; and public venues where music is played, charity and private performances being exempt. Also, although it may strike some as rather anomalous for an organization concerned primarily with collecting money for the playing of records, PPL includes in its licences a clause providing for a certain proportion of time to be devoted to live performances, thus aiming to preserve employment opportunities for artists.

PPL distributes royalties about a year after its financial year-end on 31 May: 67.5 per cent to the record companies, 20 per cent to individually named artists (with which the record companies supply PPL) and 12.5 per cent to the Musicians' Union, which puts the money into a fund benefiting session musicians, special projects and promotions. In 1985 PPL received nearly £11 million from its licensees.

A successful artist might earn between £5000 and £10,000 a year from this source.

VPL is a similar organization concerned with collection and distribution of revenue from the use of videos, and it is concentrating particularly on cable usage.

PRS

The Performing Right Society acts on behalf of composers, lyricists and publishers. Its duties are to collect, allocate and distribute royalties earned for the performance of a musical work, whether it be a recorded piece played on the radio, a snippet in a television programme, a work performed at a Wembley Stadium concert or at a youth-club gig, or played on a coach trip or in a hairdresser's. The only public venues which are exempt are churches. Similar performance royalties are collected by PRS, working with foreign affiliates, from all over the world, wherever copyright laws are enforced.

PRS has been in existence since 1914, having been formed at the same time as ASCAP, the American music performing rights organization, but 63 years after SACEM, the French equivalent. (America now has three copyright organizations and Canada two.)

PRS represents more than 600,000 copyright owners all over the world. In 1985 it had 19,792 members (16,171 writers, 2436 publishers and 1185 copyright owners and successors). Fully computerized, it is an enormous operation employing about 700 staff in a large London office block.

It collects licence fees annually from every public venue which uses music, apportions this money either by a points system for every piece of music which has been played (depending on what time of day and for how long), as with large organizations such as the BBC; or on as accurate as possible a sampling of what might have been played, as in the case of bars, factories, hairdressers, shops and so on which have local radio, juke-boxes, discos, etc. where it would be virtually impossible to log every track played.

The following is a rough guide to what you could earn from the different broadcasting outlets, based on figures for 1985: from £7.73 per minute on Radios 1, 2, 3 and 4; £41.52 per minute for BBC Television; 0.05p per minute for local radio.

Copyright royalties can provide a major source of income for a successful songwriter, and if you manage to write a standard, that could provide your pension plan. If you are neither very prolific nor very successful, however, royalty income will only come in dribs and drabs.

PRS employs inspectors all over Britain to check that venues using music have a PRS licence. The number of licences currently in force, according to a recent calculation, is 17,373. How much each pays out per year depends on its relative importance and the quantity of music played. PRS has fifty different tariffs, ranging from a few pounds to thousands a year, which are paid annually according to the type of venue or the broadcasting company.

In 1985 PRS distributed over £59.8 million: 24 per cent of this came from British and Irish public performance; 37.5 per cent from British and Irish radio and TV; 33 per cent from overseas; and 5.5 per cent from investment income. In the future revenue will also be received from cable and satellite broadcasts, although the latter is likely to prove difficult to monitor satisfactorily.

PRS distributes four times a year: twice for broadcasting royalties, in April and October; and twice for performance royalties, in July and December.

You can become a member of PRS if you are a composer, lyricist or publisher, provided you satisfy certain criteria. As a writer you need three works which have either been recorded, broadcast within the past two years or performed in public on at least 12 occasions within the past two years and commercially published; or if you have had one work in the top fifty within the last 12 months; or if you have written the theme music for a film or for a series of three or more TV episodes. Your application must be accompanied by evidence of such works and also your birth certificate. An admission fee of £25 is now charged, but after that your membership is free. If your application for membership is not accepted the fee will be refunded. If it is, you will be granted, initially, provisional membership.

As a writer you will be paid all the money due to you; if you are signed with a publisher you will be sent direct the proportion agreed in your contract – which will be no less than 50 per cent of royalties earned and should be around the 60-70 per cent mark. PRS actually prefers new writers to become members themselves as it saves it having to divide up the money.

Although you will lose half, or possibly less, of your royalties by claiming through a publisher, doing so could be to your advantage if you have written only one or two works which earn you royalties, on which you would not be entitled to claim on your own account. And a publisher, of course, should be doing more than just collecting these royalties.

Obviously it is of vital importance to notify PRS of any musical works of yours that might earn royalties: if you do not have a publisher or if you have been commissioned specially to write for a film, television or radio programme, etc., you do this using forms obtained from PRS. You must make sure that all titles and other information are correct, otherwise the royalties due to you may not be picked up by the computer.

Useful addresses

Audio/Visual Directory
Maclaren Publishers Ltd
PO Box 109
19 Scarbrook Road
Croydon
Surrey
CR9 1QH
01-688 7788
The most recent (1986) directory costs £18 inclusive of p. and p.

Billboard Publications
71 Beak Street
London W1
01-439 9411
Distributors of *This Business of Music* by Sidney Shemel and M. William Krasilovsky: £17.50 inclusive of p. and p.

British Academy of Songwriters, Composers and Authors
148 Charing Cross Road
London
WC2H 0LB
01-240 2823

British Film Institute
127 Charing Cross Road
London WC2
01-437 4355

British Phonographic Industry Ltd
Roxburghe House
273-287 Regent Street
London
W1R 7PB
01-629 8642

Gallup
202 Finchley Road
London
NW3 6BW
01-794 0461

Mechanical Copyright Protection Society
Elgar House
41 Streatham High Road
London
SW16 1ER
01-769 4400

Musicians' Union
60-62 Clapham Road
London
SW9 0JJ
01-582 5566

The Music Publishers' Association
7th floor
Kingsway House
103 Kingsway
London
WC2B 6QX
01-831 7591

The Music Week Directory
Morgan-Grampian plc
Royal Sovereign House
40 Beresford Street
London
SE18 6BQ
01-854 2200
Subscription rate (1987): £12.50.

Nu-Line Promotions
The Nomis Complex
45-53 Sinclair Road
London
W14 0NS
01-602 9407

Performing Right Society
29-33 Berners Street
London
W1P 4AA
01-580 5544

Phonographic Performance (PPL) and Video Performance (VPL)
Ganton House
14-22 Ganton Street
London
W1V 1LB
01-437 0311

PROFESSIONAL SERVICES

The following list of accountants, lawyers, manufacturing and export companies, etc. includes some of the major specialists, but not necessarily the only ones, or the best.

Accountants

Deloitte Haskins & Sells
128 Queen Victoria Street
London
EC4P 4JX
01-248 3913

Gelfand, Rennert & Feldman
82 Brook Street
London
W1Y 1YG
01-629 7169

Lubbock Fine
3-5 Bedford Row
London
WC1R 4DB
01-242 9881

Martin Greene & Partners
42 Portland Place
London W1
01-636 8926

Stoy Hayward & Co
8 Baker Street
London W1
01-486 5888

Export

Caroline Exports Ltd
56 Standard Road
London
NW10 6ES
01-961 2919

Lasgo Exports
Unit 2
Chapmans Park Industrial Estate
378-388 High Road
London
NW10 2DY
01-459 8800

Windsong Record Exports
159 Stafford Road
Croydon
Surrey
CR0 4NN
01-680 3564

Lawyers

Clintons
6 Upper St Martin's Lane
London WC2
01-379 6080

Compton Carr
6 Dyers Buildings
Holborn
London
EC1N 2JT
01-831 6981

David Landsman & Co
4 Wimpole Street
London W1
01-636 6602

Eaton & Burley
5 St Clement's Lane
Portugal Street
London
WC2A 2HH
01-404 4002

Gentle Jayes & Co
26 Grosvenor Street
London
W1X 0BD
01-629 3304

Harbottle & Lewis
34 South Molton Street
London
W1Y 2BP
01-629 7633

John Kennedy & Co
54 York Street
London W1
01-724 4707

Lee & Thompson
Green Garden House
St Christopher's Place
London W1
01-935 4665

Russells
Regency House
1-4 Warwick Street
London
W1R 5WB
01-439 8692

Stephens Innocent
St Mary's Clergy House
2 Whitechurch Lane
London E1
01-377 0464

Pressing and distribution

Mayking Records Ltd
57 Portobello Road
London
W11 3DB
01-727 2614

Lambourne Productions
Unit 2
Orpington Trading Estate
Sevenoaks Way
Orpington
Kent
0689 70622

Lyntone Audio Reproduction
5-9 Wedmore Street
London
N19 4RU
01-263 1378

PRT (Precision Records & Tapes)
105 Bond Road
Mitcham
Surrey
CR4 3UT
01-648 7000

Record Company Services
1-3 Sedley Place
London
W1R 1HH
01-409 2336

Spartan Records
London Road
Wembley
Middlesex
HA9 7HQ
01-903 4753

The Cartel (each member company's name is italicized)

Rough Trade
(London & South East)
61 Collier Street
London
N1 9BE
01-833 2133

Revolver (South West)
The Old Malt House
Little Ann Street
Bristol 2
0272 541291

Backs (East Anglia)
St Mary's Works
St Mary's Plain
Norwich
Norfolk
NR3 3AF
0603 626221

Nine Mile (Midlands)
Lower Avenue
Leamington Spa
Warks
CV31 3NP
0926 881292

Red Rhino (North)
The Coach House
Fetter Lane
York
0904 641415

Fast Forward (Scotland)
21A Alva Street
Edinburgh
EH2 4PS
031 226 4616

Library music publishers
KPM Music
21 Denmark Street
London
WC2H 8NE
01-836 6699

Bruton Music
11 Greek Street
London
W1V 5LE
01-437 4266

Record companies, publishers, recording studios
There are far too many of these to list here: consult the *Music Week Directory*, which has the most comprehensive list.

Glossary

A & R Artists and repertoire. The A & R department of a record company looks for new performers and bands and is the first port of call for new artists seeking a recording contract.

AOR Adult-orientated rock; a term often used by radio programmers.

Bags Sleeves for singles and albums. 'Picture bags' are coloured sleeves, 'white sleeves' blank ones.

BPI The British Phonographic Industry Limited, which represents UK record companies.

Cover A secondary version of an original song.

Cutting room A workroom specially set up with machines for transferring ¼-inch tapes to lacquers.

Demo Short for 'demonstration' (tape or record). It might be a tape made for promotion purposes, to play to a booker in a pub, a manager, or A & R people, for example; or a rough recording of a song, which will eventually be turned into a finished or master disc.

Doubling Playing two instruments at one session, e.g. both acoustic and electric guitar, or making two recordings (perhaps to make the texture of the sound stronger) of the same track which are then combined.

Drum machine A synthesizer which, when programmed, produces drum patterns.

Emulator/Emax A sampling keyboard: one which you can program to reproduce any sound from a trumpet to a sheep in any pattern or key. (See *sampling*.) E-mu Systems Inc. produce some of the most common digital sampling keyboards.

Fixer Booking agent for musicians or singers.

Gaffer tape Wide, strong adhesive tape for general mending purposes and for keeping electric cables in place.

Gig A live performance.

Hype A media or 'in-business' exaggeration of an artist's worth or product; unnatural push of a record, resulting in exaggerated sales and therefore higher placing in the charts than would be recorded by normal sales. May be legal or illegal depending on methods used.

ILR Independent local radio, i.e. local commercial stations.

Lacquer An aluminium disc from which records are pressed.

Master The finished version of a single or album on tape, to be turned into vinyl, cassette or CD.

MCPS Mechanical Copyright Protection Society.

Mixing See *track (2)*.

Monitor A speaker used in a recording studio or on stage which enables musicians to hear a mix of the sound being made; nowadays earphones are sometimes used instead of a monitor.

MOR Middle-of-the-road music: that which appeals to a broad spectrum of ages and types.

MU Musicians' Union.

Overdub Recording, by one musician, of more than one track on the same song.

PA Public address system: sound system used for live performance.

Playlist A list of current singles, chosen by committee, from which Radio 1 producers choose the records for the DJs to play. Top-rated records go on the 'A' list, secondary-rated ones on the 'B' list. A similar system operates for most of the commercial stations.

Plugger The person whose job it is to obtain plays of records on radio and television.

Points Royalty percentage.

Pressing The process of making copies of an album or single on vinyl, cassette or CD.

PRS Performing Right Society.

Read Popular jargon for 'sightread'; 'reading' therefore means being able to play music at sight.

Royalties Monies (a percentage of the retail or wholesale price) received by performers from record companies on record sales; songwriters receive 'mechanical' royalties every time their songs are recorded and 'performance' royalties every time they are played or performed. Royalties also accrue from sales of sheet music, to the writer of the song or other composition.

Composers/writers receive: (1) mechanical royalties (a royalty of 6¼ per cent of the retail price of the record, exc. VAT, paid every time the work is recorded and divided between the composers credited on that record), collected and paid by MCPS (excepting certain major record companies who pay direct): if the composer/writer has a publisher the money will be paid to the publisher; if not it will be paid direct to the composer/writer; (2) performance royalties (a royalty paid every time the work is performed, the amount depending on where broadcast or performed and for how long), collected and paid by PRS direct to the composer/writer; (3) sheet-music royalties (usually 10 per cent of the retail price) paid by the publisher to the composer/writer; (4) foreign royalties (a percentage of all net royalties received by the publisher in the UK from its sub-publishers or licensees), paid by the UK publisher to the composer/writer.

Artists receive: (1) record royalties (a percentage, average 10-12 per cent, of the retail price, exc. VAT, of the record) from their record company on records sold; (2) performance royalties, collected and paid by the PPL according to the number of times the recording is broadcast (the amount is determined by what is available in the annual pool of monies available to PPL) direct to the artist.

Sampling A computerized recording of any sound – musical or non-musical – stored on a floppy disc. It can be used in any key or at any pitch by being played back on a sampling keyboard. (See *emulator*.)

Showcase A 'pretend' gig, usually given in a rehearsal studio, for the benefit of people within the business (often A & R people).

Synthesizer (popularly 'synth') A machine which when programmed can reproduce a wide variety of sounds by electronic means.

Track (1) Popular name for a recorded number. (2) A band width on magnetic tape: a domestic ¼-inch tape will normally have two tracks on it, whereas a studio 2-inch tape might have 24 tracks. In recording, each track is used for a different instrument or voice, so that the various recorded tracks can be balanced and a good two-track stereo sound produced (this process is called mixing).

Index